THE ZEAL
OF HIS HOUSE

Five Generations of Lutheran Church—Missouri Synod History (1847-1972)

ELDON WEISHEIT

Publishing House
St. Louis   London

Unless stated otherwise, all photos courtesy of Concordia Historical Institute.

Concordia Publishing House, St. Louis, Missouri
Concordia Publishing House Ltd., London, E. C. 1
Copyright © 1973 Concordia Publishing House
Library of Congress Catalog Card No. 72-76988
ISBN 0-570-03516-3
MANUFACTURED IN THE UNITED STATES OF AMERICA

To

**Those who have joined
The Lutheran Church — Missouri Synod
as adults**

**In appreciation of your contributions
to the heritage of the synod**

CONTENTS

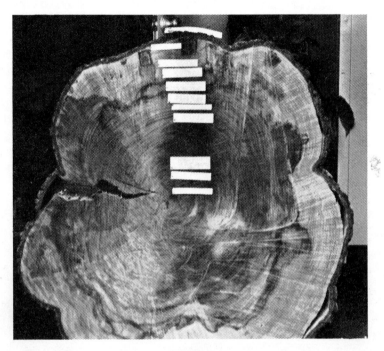

1847 Tree

A cross section of a tree that sprouted in 1847 correlates the history of the Synod and the United States. The Synod was founded when the U. S. was fighting the Mexican war in 1847. In 1865 the Civil War ended, and the Synod sent out its first traveling missionaries. The teachers college opened in River Forest the same year the Panama Canal was completed (1913). "This Is the Life" started in 1952, the same year Dwight David Eisenhower became president.

I. Some History About History
(Or "Let Me Talk You into Reading the Whole Thing")

The Lutheran Church — Missouri Synod is celebrating its 125th anniversary. Well, happy birthday. Now what?

It might seem that the 125th anniversary of a church body (which after all isn't limited by three score and 10 as we mortals are) is not so important. Not unimportant but more like a 17th or 29th wedding anniversary. Not a big deal.

But there are some good reasons for three million people (that's about how many belong to the Missouri Synod) to take time out to appreciate the history of their church body.

Reason No. 1: If the celebration were held only every 50 years to save all the energy and cash for one big party, every other generation would miss out on an opportunity to become more aware of church history. You were either very young when the synod celebrated its centennial in 1947, or you will be among the more senior of the senior citizens when it (God willing) celebrates its 150th birthday in 1997. A celebration every 25 years more or less hits every generation.

Reason No. 2: This will be the first opportunity for two out of three members of the Synod to celebrate a church anniversary. Total membership of the Missouri Synod has more than doubled since 1947. Add to that the figure that one third of those who belonged to the church in 1947 have now joined the church in heaven and have been replaced by new members, and you can see that most members of the church today are new and may have little identity with denominational history.

Two reasons explain why there are so many new church members. The birthrate in the United States and Canada has been high during the last 25 years. Lutheran families have done their share to contribute to the high birthrate. Most of our children remain in the church. It is possible that the pastor or teacher of your congregation may have been born in 1947 or later. The immigration rate in Canada has also been high during the last quarter century. Many new Lutherans have come to Canada (and some to the U. S.) from Europe and are now members of the Missouri Synod.

Another important reason for growth during the last 25 years of our synod is an expanded interest in evangelism. Though our track record of gaining new members has always been high when compared with other church bodies, there has been an increased interest in many congregations for organized evangelism programs.

All of these new members (children born in church families, immigrants from Europe, and adult converts) are taught the doctrines of the church. But seldom do they have a chance to learn the history of their church body. Some families have belonged to the Missouri Synod for five or six generations. But those are rare. Only a small percentage of the present membership of the Synod are descendants of the original 4,000 members in 1847. Yet all the young and the new members are equally a part of the synod.

One of the purposes of this anniversary celebration is to help us understand the church family. By rummaging through the old church albums we will find both the family skeletons and the family treasures. We will share some of the sorrows and frustrations of those who have worked to keep the synod going for 125 years and we will share some of their joys and successes. But most important, we will see how we are a part of that family.

That brings up one more issue that I should discuss with you before we plunge into the history part. The first part of Missouri Synod history is heavy with the German influence. If you are German but not a Saxon or Franconian (I'm neither), you might feel that you are on the edge of the stage. If you're not German at all, you might feel you missed the whole scene. But it's not so!

If the synod had remained a combination of Saxons and Franconians, there would not be much to celebrate today. From the very beginning it expanded and incorporated people of other backgrounds into its mainstream. It is the influence of people of many backgrounds that has been added to the influence of the founding fathers that gives us something worth celebrating today.

Reason No. 3: Another good reason for making a big deal of the 125th anniversary is that it gives us a chance to evaluate the people and events of our church history in the light of the world in which we live.

Maybe that needs explaining. Some people view history as a closed subject. In that view, once names and dates and events are recorded in a book, the history is complete. All one has to do to keep history up to date is to dust off the old book and add the latest chapter.

But there is another view of history (it's the one I'm pushing) that sees history as alive and as a part of the world today. This view says an act of history is not completed when it is recorded. Instead, an event that may have happened long ago started something that continues as long as that event is history.

An example: In 1517 Martin Luther, with the help of some others who were on his side and with some motivation coming from some others who were not on his side, started what we now call the Protestant Reformation. Books have recorded the names, dates, and events that tell us what happened back then. Yet new books are still being written on the subject of the Reformation today. People still debate some of the issues of that day and see the influence of the Reformation on other current events. The conflicts of that day are often studied to help us understand our own. The history of over 455 years ago is still alive because it is still related to what we are now doing.

There were other people doing other things on other days 455 years ago. But what they did is not history for us. It is not history not only because we don't know about it, but also because it is not important to us. Events become history not only because they are done but because they do something.

Our purpose in studying the history of the Missouri Synod is not to make either heroes or villains of those who have worked in the church. We do not intend to examine our record to show how great we are or to purge ourselves by admitting how often we have failed.

Instead we will study history to understand ourselves and to see how we got to where we are today, so we can have a better understanding about where we are going. The events that have occurred during the last 125 years in the Missouri Synod which are important to us today are those that influence us today. During those years the governments and societies under which we live have also added 125 years to their history. We need to understand how the societies have influenced the church and the church the societies. During those 125 years other Christian denominations have been born, died, or grown 125 years older. We are related to them. As relatives our behavior has affected them and theirs us. We need to know about it.

The history of our church as we see it in 1972 is different than it was seen in 1947. We know that those who live in 1997 will also see the history in a different way. History is not an exact science in which both the questions and answers have already been provided. History is alive with all the vitality and all the conflict that life has. Any study of history is not an attempt to box it in and confine the experiences of the past. Rather the effort is to open history up so the reader can see his or her place in it.

Reason No. 4: There is a special reason for this particular history book at this time. I write it not as a church historian but as a parish pastor who somehow got involved in writing. There are several great historians and many good historians in our church today. They are studying the history of the past and recording the history of the present in the proper scholarly way.

This "pastoral approach to history" is just skimming the cream off the work of the real historians. The book is directed to church members who have little or no knowledge of church history. Hopefully it will whet your appetite to read more complete and more analytical histories of our synod and the church in general. A list of good books for further study is included as an appendix.

But the fact is that most church members do not get involved in a study of church history. This lighter, more personal approach is to give a basic introduction to history along with some everyday applications. Please regard me as a tour guide. I'll take you on a trip through the pages of our history and point out some things that are interesting and worthwhile. Like other tour guides I'll have to remind you that we are in a hurry and must move on. I won't emphasize names and dates but rather hope to give you a feeling for the things that happened.

By seeing how the Holy Spirit has worked in the lives of those who have gone before and by feeling how Christ changed human lives and how despite human weaknesses and both petty and grand selfishness on the part of people the Gospel still came through, may the generation of 1972 be encouraged to know that the same Spirit can work in them. That's us, you and me.

II. A Little Bit About a Lot of Old Church Problems
(Or "The Itch That Started All the Scratching")

You know, of course, that the Missouri Synod didn't start at a convention or a committee meeting. And that no one ever said, "Hey, let's get a bunch of guys together and start the Missouri Synod."

Trying to find the moment when it was determined that such a church body as ours would be formed is a fruitless and needless task. We'll talk about the founding convention in 1847 later on, but that wouldn't have happened had not other things occurred first. Assuming that the whole thing started in 1847 is like thinking a baby was born when no one was pregnant. Many factors contributed to the circumstances that led a group of people to unite in what we now know as the Missouri Synod.

The point is that the beginning of the Missouri Synod was not the initiation of something new but a continuation of something that has been around a long time — namely, the holy Christian church. To find the real beginning we'd have to march back through the Reformation times of the 16th century and wade through the Dark Ages that began a thousand years ago to reach the real beginning on the first Christian Pentecost. It was then that promises of the Old Testament and of Christ were fulfilled, and the Holy Spirit tuned in on the people who were the founders of the Christian church.

Many chapters and volumes of church history had already been recorded before the term Lutheran (let alone Missouri Synod) made the scene. Without these earlier chapters there would be no meaning to the history we are now studying. Space allowed for this project and its purpose will not allow a rerun of all the earlier events. Be aware of the earlier history. Maybe later on you should do some reading about the earlier history too.

We pick up the story in the early part of the 19th century in Northern Europe in an area we will call Germany for the sake of convenience. Actually Germany as a country didn't make the maps until later on. In the early 1800s that part of the world was a group of small states each independent in some ways yet with an awareness of a shared culture and a dream of federation and union.

Religion was part of the problem—and part of the cure. The fragmentation of countries that had occurred was a part of the political quakes that followed the Reformation 300 years earlier. After the theological struggles of the Reformation a long series of political wars spread across Europe. Without the authority of the Holy Roman Empire, which had for generations been only a political shadow with authority that existed only as long as it was not challenged, much of Europe was divided into warring city states. On the surface this struggle in Northern Europe was between three Christian groups: The Roman Catholic, the Evangelicals (that is, Lutherans), and the Reformed.

In reality much of the fighting in "religious" wars was a struggle to fill the vacuum that had developed in political authority. As princes and kings were able to establish their leadership over groups, a type of peace was established on the basis of "The religion of the prince is the religion of the people."

Though there were continued religious persecutions by all parties, the establishment of state approved religions allowed the migration of those with deep religious feelings (and outward conversion of those without it). Again religion and government lived in harmony as it had under the old Holy Roman Empire. And again the political clout of princes became the primary means of maintaining religion.

Naturally, strong leaders attempted to combine small states into larger ones to expand their own authority. In 1817 King Frederick William III established the Prussian Union. To create a political unity in his country he also had to establish a religious unity between Lutheran and Reformed churches.

Because both church bodies had accepted the protection of the government they were also under the control of political power. Through a series of proclamations, often issued in the name of religious freedom, the king decreed that no congregation could withhold its ministry from anyone. By law Lutheran congregations had to baptize, commune, marry, and bury Reformed Christians. And the Reformed congregations had to extend the same privileges to Lutherans. Differences in the teachings of the two church bodies were ignored.

A political solution to the church's problem of division was possible because the church had entered a period of rationalism. Maybe we ought to take a short side trip to expand on the subject of rationalism. (We shall do this a bit later, below:)

Because the Reformation had made everyone brush up on theology, it was followed by a period in which great emphasis was placed on doctrine – not only among Lutherans and Reformed as they spelled out their place in the church, but also among the Roman Catholics. For the first time since the early centuries new creeds and statements of faith were written and circulated. Each group clearly spelled out its own position, and by comparing their creeds with the other statements of faith they became convinced that they were right and the others were wrong.

In the generations that followed, each group became more entrenched in its rightness and the other groups' wrongness. Orthodox doctrine became the test of true religion. The problem was that orthodoxy continued to refight only the issues of the Reformation (that's where the issues had been spelled out), and the church became more and more remote from the lives of the people. Doctrine became something that was used to show others how they were wrong rather than to share and to strengthen faith. Faith became a matter of being right rather than being committed to a living Christ. Not all Christians followed orthodoxy to these extremes.

It is easy to understand why people got bored with such orthodoxy. As in the times before the Reformation, theology was in control of the learned professors and the great universities. Many people and parish pastors and eventually the theologians reacted against the misuse of theology by what came to be known as dead orthodoxy.

One reaction to the overemphasis on orthodoxy was Pietism – in which doctrine was not considered important. Pietism put the attention on leading a good life and having the right emotional reactions. Pietists wanted to avoid not only evil but any possibility of being associated with evil. They developed strict moral codes for their own lives and felt that the same standards should be accepted by others as a part of the Christian faith.

Another reaction to the overload of orthodoxy was rationalism, which was the big thing in Northern Europe in the early 1800s.

Rationalism is, as its title suggests, based on human reason. While reacting against a rigid use of Biblical authority and doctrinal statements, those who accepted rationalism turned to a natural religion based on man's ability to figure things out for himself. There were different degrees and different phases of rationalism; in general it ignored the authority of Scripture and made human reason the top authority. While rationalism always accepted the existence of God, He was seen as a distant power. Christ became only a man: a great teacher or a good example. Some interesting cases of extreme rationalism are recorded. Some ministers ceased to baptize in the name of the Father, Son, and Holy Spirit but made a new trinity—they baptized in the name of reason, logic, and goodness.

In these brief and incomplete explanations of orthodoxy, Pietism, and rationalism, please understand that not all was evil in any of them. Each was an overreaction to previous problems. Each had followers who became overly enthusiastic about "the cause" and failed to see the big picture. And, important point, each was begun to cure a serious problem in the church.

We've spent all this time on a historical once-over for two reasons: First, with this background you can understand some of the strong views of the early leaders of the Missouri Synod. Remember, they were reacting to the problems of their world, not ours. Most were educated in European universities that were heavy with rationalism. They chafed under the political authority of the Prussian Union.

Second, it is easier for us to be objective about the theological problems of two centuries ago than it is about our own difficulties. But by looking at actions and reactions of that period and by seeing that sometimes they solved problems by creating new problems we can better understand the trends of our own time.

III. The Migration to America
(Or "Have Theology — Will Travel")

Now that the stage is set for Act I of "The Story of the Missouri Synod" let's introduce the cast of characters. The first act will be divided into three scenes for the three groups that eventually organized the Missouri Synod.

Scene I: The Loehe Men

The largest bloc of clergy involved not only in the founding of the synod but also active in its early years were a group called the Loehe men (that title will be explained later). In less than 10 years 100 Lutheran pastors and theological students, classified as Loehe men, migrated from Germany to America.

This mass movement of ministers started as a trickle: one man, Fredrick K. D. Wyneken (say Win-e-kin). Wyneken was born in Bavaria in 1810 and was educated in German universities. Like other theological students of his time he was subjected to the glories of rationalism. When he was 28 years old, by then an ordained Lutheran pastor, he came to the United States.

Wyneken later said that he had no deep theological reason for leaving Germany. Although he had been taught the glories of rationalism, he apparently was not greatly impressed by the theology of reason. He did not shake the theological dust off his feet as he left Germany as the Saxons (Scene II) did later. Nor did he come to America with dreams of saving the Indians as the Franconians did (Scene III). Wyneken had a spirit of adventure. Coming to America was the thing to do.

Yet Wyneken came across the water as a Lutheran minister and had every intention of remaining a Lutheran minister. When he arrived in Baltimore in 1838, he contacted a local Lutheran congregation. If he had any illusions about the Lutherans in America being more pure than those in Europe they were soon shattered. After his first

17

PASTOR WYNEKEN

PASTOR STEPHAN

worship service in a Lutheran church in Baltimore he said, "I don't know if it was of God or the devil, but it certainly wasn't Lutheran."

However, Wyneken did not let his concerns about the inadequacies of American Lutheranism prevent him from going to work. He headed west to the pioneer country of Ohio, Indiana, and Michigan. He was shocked to find large numbers of German Lutherans without pastoral care. Because Lutherans were used to an educated and ordained clergy groups of German Lutherans had not organized their own congregations.

As Wyneken worked on the frontier two things happened to him. First, he became more and more conservative in his own theology. In his earlier congregations he had served Communion to Lutheran and Reformed alike and did not seem concerned with strict Lutheran doctrine. But as time went on he felt the need for more clear teaching of Scriptural truths. Second, he saw that there was far too much work for the available ministers. Already he was becoming disillusioned with his own synod and the General Synod. He requested help from the General Synod and the Pennsylvania Ministerium but they were not able to supply more pastors. He wrote to friends in Germany and was able to get a teacher and several missionaries to come, but that was not enough.

In 1841 Wyneken went back to Germany because of his poor health and because he wanted to recruit missionaries to America. He had

18

just gotten married a few months before, so he now went on a honeymoon.

Wyneken received little encouragement in Germany until he met Pastor Wilhelm Loehe (say Lay-he) of Neuendettelsau, Bavaria. Loehe understood Wyneken's concerns and started recruiting pastors for the mission field. Though Loehe himself never came to the United States, he had a great influence on American Lutheranism. He is a cofounder of two Lutheran synods in America and one seminary.

The Loehe men came to the United States and joined existing synods—mostly the Ohio and Michigan. But the supply of pastors still did not fill the demand.

Wyneken returned to the United States in 1843. While in Germany his theology had become more conservative. He had written several articles against the General Synod. He spoke against the unionistic practices (that is worshiping together with other denominations) of the General Synod. In 1844 Wyneken, then serving a congregation in Baltimore, was a delegate to the General Synod. Again he made a plea for the synod to return to the Lutheran Confessions. When his requests were not granted, he and his congregation resigned from the synod.

The curtain drops on Scene I at a time of frustration and disappointment.

Scene II: the Saxon Migration

The largest group of Germans who came to America and helped form the Missouri Synod were the Saxons. Though the Loehe men provided more pastors, the Saxons had more people.

Often the story of the Saxons has been told as though they were the only stream to flow into Missouri. This is not true. It is the contribution of each of the three early groups and the continued input of others later on rather than the importance of one group that helped build a strong Missouri Synod. Perhaps their part in the founding has gotten more attention because they were part of both the state and the synod called Missouri. They were always near influential parts of the synod—Concordia Seminary and Concordia Publishing House, for example, and for the last several decades synodical headquarters have been in St. Louis.

Or maybe their story became important because it is an exciting story—filled with dreams and ideals, conflict and scandal—all the makings of an exciting novel.

But the purpose of relating the story of the Saxons is not just to share the adventure of a good story. The basic importance of the Saxon migration is that it shows the struggles to redefine the church on American soil. The human weaknesses and strengths as seen in the Saxon story show the power of the Spirit working through people. Though they were certainly unaware of it, this small band of immigrants, who made a mess out of many things, also made a great contribution to the structure of all Lutheranism in the United States and Canada, and through the mission work of North American groups they have influenced the whole world.

The story starts with Martin Stephan — at last a name that can be pronounced. Stephan's parents had been Roman Catholics but converted to Lutheranism and raised Martin in the Lutheran Church and for the Lutheran ministry. In 1810 Stephan accepted a call to St. John Congregation in Dresden, Saxony.

St. John was an unusual congregation. It belonged to the state church, making its pastor a civil servant. But the congregation was "Bohemian" meaning it served a group of Lutherans from Bohemia (part of today's Czechoslovakia) with special permission to follow their own worship patterns. That special privilege gave Stephan more freedom than most state church ministers had.

Stephan was a powerful preacher. His sermons were always centered on justification by faith in Jesus Christ. He encouraged Bible study and stressed the need to return to the old Lutheranism. A Lutheran from America visited his congregation in 1827 and reported in the *Lutheran Observer:*

> His [Stephan's] sermon was plain, vigorous, and evangelical, and well calculated to enlighten the mind and affect the heart. There was nothing like an attempt to show off . . . no effort for applause — nothing of the kind . . . . holding up Jesus Christ as the only hope of a perishing world and demanding faith in Him.

Stephan attracted the attention of many people — especially the youth. His congregation grew rapidly. Within 10 years it had six times as many members as when Stephan arrived. Young theological students were impressed by Stephan's sermons.

But success had its problems. The members of St. John Congregation were not particularly pleased at having their church filled with outsiders. Neighboring pastors resented their members crossing parish lines to hear Stephan. Government officials recognized Stephan as a threat.

There were a number of personal attacks against Stephan. He wisely ignored them and continued his preaching — until about 1823 when he began to defend himself. He would occasionally speak of leaving Saxony because of its corruptness. Though he continued to be a faithful pastor, his emphasis gradually became less a return to old Lutheranism and became instead the development of Stephanism. Looking back it is easy to see that Stephan's enemies succeeded in getting him away from his original message to a new position of defending himself. Though confessional Lutheranism was still the title on the program, his actions brought more attention to himself.

A group of young clergy, many of whom were later to be the founders of Missouri Synod, formed around Stephan. They needed him for guidance; he needed them for moral support. He was a generation and a half older than any of them. They held secret meetings at night (against the law) and discussed migration to England, America, or Australia. As he went to and from such meetings Stephan was often in the company of young adults, both men and women. He was criticized for this and several charges of sexual crimes were placed against him.

His followers read such harassment as evidence of his rightness. In the eyes of many he became a martyr for the truth of confessional Lutheranism. The adoration given him by his followers raised the anger level of those who were against him. The local police raided his home and church—and found nothing against him. He was spied upon. The unquestioning love of his followers and the unrelenting hatred of his opponents added to making the Stephan personality the issue of the day.

In 1836 the attacks against Stephan increased. A group of pastors met with Stephan to make plans to leave Saxony. They listed lay people who they thought would be willing to form a colony of confessional Lutherans in America. Scouts were sent to the U. S. to find a place. Florida and Georgia were ruled out because of the heat. Ohio was too crowded. Missouri was accepted because its climate and land were similar to that of Saxony.

Originally the leaders planned a colony of 100 people. But as word about the plans spread more and more people asked to join. The migration was preached as a last-ditch effort to save the Lutheran Church from rationalism. Stephan became the Noah of his day as he collected those who would board his ark before the floods of human reason took over.

Government opposition became even stronger. Stephan was arrested—again on a morals charge. Pious Lutheran ministers gleefully broke the law as they organized the migration. Divorces were arranged for those who wanted to go without a spouse. Two of the young clergy, the Walther brothers, took their orphaned niece against the will of her legal guardian. The mother of another minister sat in jail rather than reveal where the niece was. The people who led the migration saw it as a matter of saving souls.

The number of those who wanted to join the colony rose daily and eventually came near 800. Five ships were chartered in the early winter of 1838 to leave from Bremen. (In case you remember the names of the *Niña, Pinta,* and the *Santa Maria,* you will also want to know that the Saxon ships were the *Johann Georg, Copernicus, Olbers, Republic,* and the *Amalia.*) Though the original members of the colony were loyal Stephanites filled with a zeal to preserve the faith, many of the later followers were more interested in finding a way to America. All but two, who paid their way as passengers, joined the colony and contributed their money, if they had any, to the common treasury. The colony had a common fund of over $80,000 when they left. No one was refused because he had no money. (Salvation can neither be bought with money nor denied to those without money.)

Stephan, by this time a grandfather, left his wife and seven of their eight children in Dresden. Three of the children were deaf mutes. The son who came with him, also a Martin, was a teen-ager. It is to the credit of the state church of Saxony that it granted Frau Stephan a pension.

The ships sailed from Europe in early October 1838 and took an average of 60 days to arrive in New Orleans — except for the *Amalia,* the smallest of the five, which was lost at sea. There were rough storms at the time, and it is assumed the water overpowered it.

There is a legend about the *Amalia* worth recording. Prior to leaving Saxony Stephan discussed the future church organization in America with his fellow clergy. They all assumed that they would follow the European system of having bishops. They also all assumed who that bishop would be — anyway, let's say the crown was the same size as Stephan's hat. The group had bought, from the common fund, proper vestments for a bishop. The expensive purchases were well publicized in the German papers. While at sea one of the other ships was stopped and searched by Swedish pirates who took nothing. When the Saxons finally realized their friends on the *Amalia* were dead (they didn't give up hope until after May 1839), they wondered if the pirates had been looking for the bishop's vestments and had later found them on another ship.

Another interesting fact about the *Amalia* (by the way, it carried the two paying passengers) is that it was insured by the Saxons, as were the other ships. This is curious in the light of the later considerable Missouri Synod opposition against insurance of any kind (which came about largely because of the nefarious activities of the companies).

One more *Amalia* story: There are still those in the Missouri Synod who say the Synod's problems will be solved when the people on the *Amalia* get here—'cause they're walking in.

While we've got all the Saxons crossing the Atlantic, let's take time to mention the problem of numbers—of Saxons, that is. There are several sets of statistics on the migration. These differences are caused not only by inadequate records (and the use of initials for either titles or names—P. Schmitt could be Peter Schmitt or Pastor Schmitt) but also by the situation when the count was taken. About 700 left Germany on the five ships; about 60 were on the *Amalia*. A few Saxons stayed in New Orleans. Then some other Germans who were already in St. Louis joined the colony. A few came via New York—including the pastor's mother who had sat it out in jail because she wouldn't tell where Walther had hidden his niece. A few months later approximately 100 more came in a second migration—also via New York. Add a few births and a few deaths and a few dropouts along the way, and you see why the figure changed frequently.

Basically it was a young group—average age 25. There were few small children but a lot of young, single adults. The colony was top-heavy with clergy; 29, counting candidates and teachers. The group as such was never all in one place at one time. The nearest they came to being a unified group was when they first arrived in St. Louis—but the late group hadn't arrived yet, and they lived in various places with little opportunity to function as a unit. When the major part of the group moved to Perry County, about 100 elected to stay in St. Louis.

Stephan made the trip aboard the *Olbers*. He had to jump bond back in Dresden to make the trip. On the same ship were four of the more influential pastors: O. H. Walther and his younger brother, C. F. W., G. H. Loeber and E. G. W. Keyl. Also aboard were two of the more capable laymen: C. E. Vehse and F. A. Marbach, a lawyer.

As the *Olbers* neared New Orleans on January 14, 1839, the pastors and people invested Stephan as their bishop. There was nothing unusual about Lutherans having a bishop. However, this particular event was bound to raise a few questions:

1. Why should only one shipload of colonists be involved in such an important decision? Why not wait until they all arrived in Missouri?

The reason may have been that when he arrived they wanted Stephan to have the honored position to impress the natives.

2. What did it mean to be a bishop? In other circles a bishop was a part of the leadership of a church, a bishop among bishops. But Stephan became a bishop unto himself. The German church would never have given him such an honor.

3. What was the authority of those who signed his investiture? They were not even parish pastors, having left their congregations without proper dismissals. The immigrants had not formed congregations and had not called pastors. To give themselves some status they signed the investiture with such impossible sounding titles as "formerly pastor of . . . ."

An additional problem developed when the group with which Stephan traveled was on the way up the Mississippi River. O. H. Walther signed a document "Pledge of Subjection to Stephan" and presented it to all the others. Though some of the Saxon leaders objected to the document at the time, no one objected later when the group arrived in St. Louis and all lived under the authority of Stephan. The investiture and "Pledge of Subjection" gave Stephan authority over the Saxons in both temporal and spiritual affairs. Some have accused Stephan of demanding such power. Others say the Saxons forced the role of total leadership upon him so he would carry the full responsibility for the success or failure of the migration.

Now we're ready to let the river boats dock in St. Louis with their loads of German Lutheran immigrants. The St. Louis population was about 16,000, a frontier city. Martin Van Buren was president of the United States. The country was beginning to recover from the panic of 1837. Morse had recently invented the telegraph, and General Sam Houston had avenged the Alamo by defeating Santa Anna at the Battle of San Jacinto River.

But the Saxons were unaware of the developments in American history. They were faced with the immediate problem of housing. An appropriate house was rented for their new bishop. Other, less prestigious houses were rented, not for families, but for large groups. The Americans welcomed them and treated them well. For 2 months the colony held worship services in a public school. Then Christ Episcopal Congregation opened their building to the German Lutherans, where they continued to worship until Trinity Congregation built their first structure in 1842.

But not everyone rolled out the red carpet. A German newspaper in St. Louis made frequent attacks against the Saxons—especially

24

against Stephan. The paper used every means to demoralize the Saxons and to discredit them in the eyes of the public. There was one other Lutheran congregation in the city, but they wanted little to do with the conservative Saxons. The feeling was mutual.

Immediately after their arrival the leaders began looking for land on which they could establish their colony. One newspaper suggested they buy land from the Mormons who were about to be chased out of western Missouri. And a site only 15 miles west of St. Louis was available at a reasonable price. Apparently Stephan wanted to locate in a more remote and less tempting area. Finally the colony purchased 4,475 acres in Perry County, about 110 miles south of St. Louis via the Mississippi, for $9,234.25. It was and is a beautiful rolling country-side with many trees—similar to the Saxons' homeland. Some, but not much, of the land had already been cleared by farmers. There were several buildings on the land—the only ones still standing today were slave quarters prior to the Saxons' arrival. There was also a Lutheran church (English speaking) in the county but not on the land purchased for the colony.

Detailed plans were made for the development of the new purchase. Cities were planned and named after hometowns back in Germany. Stephanburg was to have been built on the highest hill, with a view of the farmland and the river. It would have been an impressive sight, but it was never built. Many small towns were begun, but they no longer exist. Wittenberg, on the river near the Saxons' landing place, is still there, with a population of less than a dozen. Altenburg and Frohna are now clean, small towns with large Lutheran churches and schools. A metal rod marking the center of Altenburg can still be seen in the parking lot of Trinity Lutheran Church. The community was planned with the church in the center.

As the immigrants prepared to move to their new home Stephan became more and more remote from the people. He seldom preached, and when he did he lacked his previous emphasis on justification. Instead he criticized his followers for their lack of spirituality and accused them of mistreating him. He wore his title of bishop as a cross that they had placed upon him.

The Saxons also began to find fault with their bishop. They saw him living in what they thought of as luxury while they had minimal physical comforts. More and more suspicions were voiced about the use of their common fund. They also chafed at Stephan's instructions to build bridges, roads, and churches in Perry County before homes were erected.

In May 1839 Stephan went to Perry County to inspect work being done. While he was gone, two women, still living in St. Louis, came to G. H. Loeber—each without the knowledge of the other. Each confessed to having had improper relations with Stephan. Another separately confessed that Stephan had suggested an improper relationship with her, but she had refused. Loeber discussed the situation with the other pastors still in St. Louis. In Germany such charges had been brushed off as harassment—an attempt to destroy a man of God. But in St. Louis the accusations were seen in a different light. Other factors had changed the colonists' views of Stephan. Now they were willing to believe that their leader was doing wrong.

Walther went to Perry County, though no one was to leave Saint Louis without Stephan's permission. Walther did not confront Stephan, though his presence made it obvious to all that something was wrong. First Walther told the other pastors in Perry County of the confessions. Then he tested his own leadership level with the colonists by giving orders contradicting those of Stephan. The people obeyed Walther. Stephan had announced that he would preach on Sunday. Walther announced that he would preach at the same time in a different place. The tension had become so great that only two or three showed up to hear Stephan. It was time for a showdown.

Walther made the accusations against Stephan public. Though Stephan denied any immoral conduct, no one spoke up in his defense. No legal charges were placed against Stephan before either civil or church authorities. Stephan was assumed to be guilty. He was given three choices: (1) go back to Germany, (2) be turned over to civil authorities in St. Louis, or (3) be given $100 in cash and rowed across the Mississippi River to Illinois. He took number three, the short ride to Illinois. The next day he was deposited at a place called Devil's Bake Oven on the Illinois side of the River. (A footnote to history: The largest pipeline bridge in the world now crosses the Mississippi at the same place. Those who go to view the present-day architectural wonder, are also seeing the site of the lowest point in the life of both Stephan and the Saxon immigrants.)

To conclude the story of Stephan, who was 62 years old at the time, before we see what happened to the Saxon colony: Louise Guenther, who had been his housemaid even back in Germany and who had admitted having a sexual relationship with Stephan, "escaped" 16 days later and joined him in Illinois. Stephan was pastor for a small group of Lutherans in Kaskaskia, Ill., until the community was destroyed by a flood. He then served a small German congregation of "Lutheran

26

Scene of the Saxons' arrival in Perry County on Brazeau Creek, a short distance from the Mississippi River. A plaque was placed on the rock as a memorial of the landing at a special service on Oct. 29, 1972.

One of the few buildings left that were standing in Perry County when the Saxons arrived in 1839. Formerly a slave's home, the building is now a part of the Saxon Lutheran Memorial at Frohna.

Methodists" in Horse Prairie, Ill. He became their pastor and instructed them in confessional Lutheran doctrine. The congregation later became a part of the Missouri Synod.

Stephan still claimed to be innocent. He threatened to sue the Saxons. He came back to Perry County several times, but no one would speak to him. He died in 1846 and was buried at the church he served near Redbud, Ill. Years later the Horse Prairie congregation and a group of Missouri Synod pastors in the area bought a stone for his grave.

Stephan's son Martin remained in Perry County for a while and then returned to Europe for his education. However, he came back to the United States and attended Concordia Seminary, St. Louis, while C. F. W. Walther was its president. The younger Stephan became a pastor in the Missouri Synod. His descendants have produced 10 pastors and many active laymen for the synod to which the elder Stephan had contributed much.

In the years that followed Stephan was blamed for every fault and every failure of the Saxon migration. Those who had loved him so much could not forget their emotions, so they had to turn against him. After those who had been directly involved with Stephan passed from the synodical scene, Missouri Synod histories tended to omit Stephan's downfall. Out of respect to his descendants and to the congregation at Horse Prairie, Stephan's story was dropped from history.

In the objective light of 125 years of history, Stephan can be seen as both a heroic and tragic figure. He was heroic in his defense of the Gospel and in his organizational ability as he planned the migration. His personal tragedy started when his enemies succeeded in making him defend himself, and the issue of "Stephanism" became the center of the debate. As with other figures in Biblical and church history, Stephan's strengths and his weaknesses must both be seen in the light of the Christ who has worked marvelous things through the lives of sinful people.

Meanwhile back in Perry County: The Saxons were in a state of shock. Their leader was disgraced. No matter how they blamed Stephan among themselves, in the eyes of the public they shared his humiliation. Their money was gone. They owned acres of tree covered hills that were beautiful but not ready for serious farming. The summer heat sapped their strength. Disease and depression took their toll.

Yet they went on. Not long after Stephan left, leaders of the group announced the beginning of Concordia College that was later to be Concordia Seminary. The school opened in 1839 with 11 students. Later the school was to become one of the largest seminaries in the United States, but the Saxons did not get to see that success. The students were from 5 to 15 years old. They had a one-room log school. The first teacher was in poor health and couldn't walk to the school, so they took the logs apart and reassembled them near his home.

(Later the building was moved intact to be a museum near Trinity Lutheran Church, Altenburg, where it still stands.) The school produced few ministers in its early years, but it kept going.

And so did the Saxons. Some gave up and went home. Louise Guenther's brother, a candidate for the ministry, was one of the first. Another candidate was so depressed by the experience that he left the colony, went to New York, and became a Roman Catholic. After years of warring against Lutherans through the press, he later returned to the Lutheran Church.

Another candidate, Ottomar Fuerbringer, could have gone home. Before he left Germany his mother had sown a large gold coin in the lining of his coat. It was to be a *Notpfennig,* a means of last resort (mad money in today's language), so he could return home in case things didn't work out in America. One wonders how often he fingered the coin and thought of leaving. But he took a call to a congregation in Illinois and stayed. The coin remains in the Fuerbringer family and now belongs to his grandson, Alfred, past president of Concordia Seminary, St. Louis. The family still regards the coin as another sign of God's grace—they have never had to spend their mad money.

One layman, Vehse, had previously returned to Germany because he disagreed with Stephan's rule. Another layman, Marbach, was to have an important role in the Saxons' struggle for identity. After Stephan left, the clergy took over leadership as a group. For a while it looked as though they would replace Stephan and eventually a new bishop would come from their collective leadership. But clergy and laity alike were filled with doubts. Were they still a part of the church? Had they done wrong in leaving their homeland? If Stephan were so wrong, how could they be so right? Walther and other leaders wrote confessions that were sent back to Saxony. Though they still blamed Stephan they admitted that they had been judgmental against the Saxon church, that they had wrongly separated themselves, and that they had acted in an unLutheran way. The Saxons also consulted church leaders in Sweden regarding their status in the church. But most important, they searched the Scriptures and the confessions regarding the doctrine of the church.

Free from the organization of the state church in Saxony and from the blind loyalty to Stephan, Walther and other leaders of the Saxons grew to see the church as more than their own small band of Christians. They were forced to see human weakness in the context of the church. They realized the church had to be stronger than their own limited resources. They also saw that the church was not dependent upon the authority of bishops or ordained clergy but upon the Gospel of Christ believed and shared by people. This simple but valuable lesson was to have a great influence on their future.

To settle the matter Walther and Marbach engaged in a debate in Altenburg at the college in April 1841. It seems that Marbach defended a cause that he did not believe in order to help people see the need for a new church government. Marbach spoke for a system that required clergy ordained in the tradition of apostolic succession (that is: One person properly ordained could ordain another, meaning that all clergy could trace their "ordination family" back to the apostles). Walther spoke for a concept of church as being people with the Word and sacraments—the church as those who believe in Christ. This view made the believers the authority, not the clergy. Though Walther "won," there were no hard feelings. Marbach eventually returned to his government job in Saxony, since there was little future for a German-trained lawyer in Perry County.

The curtain on Scene II lowers on a group of bewildered German immigrants in Perry County. After great tribulation they had found out that they were not God's only chosen people. Now they had to discover who they were in the church.

Everything Necessary "to a true Christian and scientific education" was taught in this log school starting in 1839.

30

PASTOR LOEHE   **REV. F. A. CRAEMER**

Scene III: The Frankenmuth Colony

Again we are back in Europe, but this time with someone you already know — Wilhelm Loehe.

Loehe had continued to serve as a recruiter for pastors and candidates to go to the U. S. as missionaries to the German speaking people. In 1844 George W. Hattstaedt was sent as a Loehe man to Michigan, where he became the pastor of Trinity Congregation in Monroe and a member of the Michigan Synod. The previous pastor of that congregation had not only worked with the German church members but also did mission work among the Chippewa Indians. During the vacancy before Hattstaedt arrived several missionaries, including J. J. F. Auch and Simon Dumser (from the Basel Institute, a European Mission society), continued the work among the Indians. Hattstaedt sent Loehe a report of efforts to share Christ with the American natives.

Loehe's main interest had been to provide pastors for Germans in the U. S. But Hattstaedt's report reminded him of the need for missionaries to Indians too. But Loehe knew that a different approach would be necessary. As Loehe considered this special mission need, two ministerial candidates, Lorenz Loesel and August Craemer, came to him and volunteered to go to America. Our major interest will be in Craemer (say Kramer), born in 1812.

31

Instead of sending the pastors as individual missionaries they developed a plan of training a colony of Christian missionaries. The colony would call a pastor and they would go as a group to live among the Indians. By their way of life they would witness to the American natives, and they could then teach them the Gospel of Christ.

Throughout the winter of 1844-1845 a small group met regularly with Loehe and Craemer. The prospective colonists included a married couple with a small child, seven bachelors, and four young ladies who were engaged to men in the group. Marriage laws made it impossible for them to be married in Germany, but the matter was taken care of as soon as they got on the boat. After months of intensive training this small group became probably one of the best trained lay mission teams the church has ever had.

On April 4, 1845, Craemer was ordained as pastor of the group, and along with three other Loehe men, they went to Bremen and boarded the *Caroline* for their trip to the new world.

About 50 other passengers were aboard the ship in addition to the mission colony and Loehe men. One of them was Dorothea Benthien who was traveling to America with her brother and sister-in-law and a 5-year-old boy, Henry. Craemer assumed that the boy was Dorothea's nephew and was greatly impressed with her concern for others on the ship—especially those who became ill during the difficult trip.

Craemer later learned that Henry was Dorothea's son and that she had never been married. But by that time he also knew her to be a good Christian woman, and her past mistake did not prevent him from falling in love with her. Before the *Caroline* arrived in New York (a 50-day trip) Craemer announced his intention to marry Dorothea. Members of his mission colony were shocked that he would even consider marrying "that kind of woman."

The trip ended on a sad note. The one child in the colony died of smallpox just before they arrived in New York. She was buried at sea.

As soon as they cleared customs, Craemer and his fiancée were united in marriage at St. Matthew Lutheran Church—the oldest Lutheran Church in the United States, founded in 1664 and later becoming a part of the Missouri Synod. When the mission colony arrived they were greeted by one of Walther's representatives in New York. It was a common practice for Lutherans who were already in America to greet newcomers to protect them from the hustlers, who often took advantage of an immigrant's ignorance. This was the first, though brief, contact between the two main groups that later helped establish the Missouri Synod.

Craemer's marriage caused difficulties in his mission colony. Tensions showed up even regarding small, unrelated issues. Members of the group began to question Craemer's leadership, which made him all the more unyielding. The hard feelings of the colonists regarding Dorothea, the strain of five honeymooning couples trying to live a communal life with a few extra bachelors around, and the sorrow of the couple whose child had died all added to the burden of the small band as they traveled to Michigan and their new home.

Missionary Auch had rented a house for them in Saginaw City, where they stayed as a group while they searched for land. Like their counterparts in Perry County they found a place that reminded them of home and purchased 680 acres for $1,700. The sight of that much money in cash (they carried it in a bucket) shocked local residents. Actually they had a fund of over $3,000 contributed by Christians back in Europe, who wanted to support their work.

While continuing to live in Saginaw City, the colonists started building their first town, Frankenmuth — meaning the courage of the Franconians and named after their home in Germany. The two Basel missionaries, Auch and Dumser, became a part of the project since they too were interested in mission work among the Indians. However, the two new men walked right into the cleavage between Craemer and the colonists.

There were disagreements about how to divide the land, how to do mission work, and, finally, a doctrinal struggle between Craemer and Auch. Craemer accused Auch of extending the privilege of the Lord's Supper to non-Lutherans. Auch accused Craemer of being a pope. Meanwhile Craemer became physically ill; this added both to his discomfort and to his insecurity as a leader.

Under such circumstances the first home was completed in Frankenmuth and the colonists moved in — except for Pastor Craemer and family because of his illness. Leaders of the colony wrote a letter to Loehe suggesting that Craemer be dismissed as their pastor and that Auch replace him. When faced with a rebellion, Craemer, whose health had improved, resolved to change his style of leadership, and a temporary peace was arranged. He moved his family to Frankenmuth. Later his stepson strayed away from the settlement. All members of the colony joined in a frantic search for the boy and found him. This act brought a reconciliation to the group. The pastor's wife and child were accepted by the others in the group. Both Auch and Dumser went on to other work.

But the residents of Frankenmuth were at a low point. Their dreams of being missionaries to the Indians were not being fulfilled. Instead of being a good example that the Indians would want to follow they had opposed one another.

Then in 1846 a second group of colonists, about 100, arrived in Michigan. Members of this group were not the well-trained missionaries wanting to share the Gospel with the Indians that the first group had been. They were colonists who helped establish a strong German Lutheran settlement that still exists today.

But what about the Indians?

The curtain drops on Scene III.

1847 Original parishes by state

IV. The Birth of the Missouri Synod
(Or "The More We Get Together the Happier We'll Be")

Each scene in Act I ended on a sad note. The transfer of the church from German to American soil was not easy. The difficulties of each group were perhaps necessary—necessary for them to come to grips with the way the church would have to operate in the new world. The pains and sorrows of each group came as they shed the dreams that had seemed possible while they were still in their native land. In America they faced a new reality and new dreams, after they had mourned the passing of the old.

Act II, the birth of the synod, begins as each group faces its new environment. They now began to look beyond themselves to see what should be done and what they could do.

The first real evidence to the world that the Saxons were going to make it after all came in September 1844 when Walther published the first issue of *Der Lutheraner* (The Lutheran. It is still being published in the German language under the same name—one of the oldest religious publications in America.) By the way, C. F. W. Walther no longer lived in Perry County. His older brother, O. H. Walther, who was the pastor of Trinity Congregation in St. Louis (made up of the colonists who never moved to Perry County), had died, and the younger Walther had become Trinity's pastor.

DR. WALTHER

Der Lutheraner, the Synod's first official periodical, was originally published under the auspices of Trinity Lutheran Church in St. Louis.

Der Lutheraner was published, not as a net to draw together all orthodox Lutherans in America into a common synod, but as an announcement that the true Christian church was still alive and well among the Saxons. Because of the bad publicity they had received the Saxons feared that their Christian witness had been lost. After they were through licking their wounds, they wanted to again become a part of the mission of the church. They still maintained their zeal for true doctrine and conservative Lutheranism. But they wanted to show this doctrine to others as evidence of their faith in Jesus Christ.

Copies of *Der Lutheraner* spread with amazing speed not only in the frontier areas of the West but also back East. Wyneken read the first issue and exclaimed, "Thank God there are other true Lutherans in America." Wilhelm Sihler, another Loehe man, rejoiced that the Saxons had recovered from the problems of Stephan's leadership. *Der Lutheraner* reintroduced the Saxons to their new neighbors. This time the meeting was more favorable.

The second event that lead to the founding of the Missouri Synod was clearly directed toward the forming of a conservative synod of Lutherans in America. Loehe in Europe had followed the activities of the Lutherans in Perry County and St. Louis. Later, in 1844 he sent a series of questions to Sihler and Adam Ernst for them to evaluate and to pass on to Walther. The questions came to Walther in December. The sixth question was: Would it not be possible to establish a synod with our brethren in the West?" — meaning that the Loehe men and the Saxons should unite. Walther answered by saying it was a good idea and offered to use *Der Lutheraner* to get the word out.

Following the May 1845 convention of the Ohio Synod, a group of Loehe men planned to meet in Cleveland later in the year to discuss the formation of a new Ohio Synod as a conservative Lutheran body. They agreed to invite F. C. D. Wyneken, who by then did not belong to any synod. Ernst also wrote to Walther — not to invite him to the meeting but to keep him posted on the events.

Walther immediately answered Ernst's letter. He encouraged the Ohio men in their plans for a new synod and gave them some advice. He suggested the new synod be based on the Word of God and the Confessions of the Lutheran Church, including, if possible, the Saxon Articles of Visitation. From his experience with other Lutherans in America Walther also suggested that the new synod have the responsibility of doctrinal supervision. Perhaps because of his experience in Germany, he also said the supervision should not be that of a higher court but of brotherly admonition. He envisioned the new synod as an advisory body through which the congregations could work together. From his own experience in the Altenburg Debate Walther also stressed that the new synod include lay delegates as voting members. — All of that as a response to a letter telling him that they were having a meeting to which he was not invited.

But Walther's advice was carefully read at the Cleveland meeting, held in September 1845. Sixteen Loehe pastors and two students were present. A. F. Craemer had planned to attend but he was ill during that time. Theodor Julius Brohm, a Saxon pastor who had moved to New York, was invited. He couldn't attend, but he sent a letter to show his interest and to keep his name on the mailing list.

The delegates agreed that they should form the new synod. But they saw that it should not be another Ohio Synod. With a wider vision they assigned three men to visit Walther in St. Louis and bring him up to date. Then they would have another meeting.

After sitting out the winter, three Loehe men (W. Sihler, A. Ernst and F. Lochner) went from Ohio to St. Louis for their meeting with Walther. By coincidence their boat stopped at Wittenberg, in Perry County, as they came up the Mississippi River. The three men recognized that the Wittenberg houses were built by Germans (even their architecture was orthodox). They also noticed that the three men who boarded the ship at Wittenberg were ministers, but assumed that they were Methodist. But they soon discovered that the men were Saxon pastors G. H. Loeber, E. G. W. Keyl, and C. F. Gruber, also headed for St. Louis and the meeting with Walther.

The meeting-by-chance of the Saxons and the Loehe men didn't get the future relationship off to a good start. The Saxons questioned the Loehe men's academic qualifications as theologians — except for Sihler who was a doctor of philosophy from a German university. The Loehe men thought the Saxons were clannish and unfriendly.

However, when they arrived in St. Louis and got down to the business of discussing the church and the establishment of a new synod for conservative Lutherans all went well. The Saxons listened to the report of the Cleveland meeting. A draft of a constitution was discussed, and copies were sent to all others who had taken a part or shown an interest in the Cleveland meeting.

Also one of the Loehe men, F. Lochner, became engaged to Walther's sister-in-law. After the others returned to Ohio, Lochner remained in Missouri long enough to get married. Thus, as two European nations became related by marriages in royal families, the Loehe men and the Saxons established their first union – by marriage. They could have coined a phrase – they were in fellowship-in-law.

The last planning meeting was held in July 1846 at Fort Wayne, Indiana. Again 16 pastors were present, and six more sent letters to show their interest. Despite Walther's insistence that the laity have a vote in the future synod, the clergy did all the planning. The Fort Wayne meeting was the first that included representation of all three major groups that were to form the synod. A. F. Craemer and W. Hattstaedt from Frankenmuth were present for the first time. All the final details for the constitution were discussed, including the name for the new synod which was to be "The German Evangelical Lutheran Synod of Missouri, Ohio, and Other States." Remembering that the name was picked at the Fort Wayne meeting helps explain why Missouri and Ohio got their names on the letterhead. Of the 22 pastors present or represented by letter, eight were from Ohio and five from Missouri. Three came from both Indiana and Illinois, two from Michigan, and one from New York. The representation was different at the founding convention the next year.

The Fort Wayne meeting made plans for the formal organization of the new synod in April of the following year. The Fort Wayne draft of the proposed constitution was printed in *Der Lutheraner* for all congregations to read and study.

Since 1847 becomes the date from which Missouri Synod counts its anniversary years, we should look briefly at the United States at that time. James Polk, America's first successful "dark horse" candidate, was president. Florida and Texas had become states in 1845. Iowa became a state, the 29th, in 1846. Wisconsin would enter the Union the following year. People were headed west on the Oregon Trail. The 49th parallel became the line between the U. S. and Canada though Polk's presidential campaign had been based on "54-40 or fight." Chicago was a small city of 20,000 people – smaller than Saint Louis at that time and difficult for the traveler to reach.

The convention began on Jubilate Sunday, April 25, 1846, with worship services and got down to business the following Monday morning. In some ways the convention was an anticlimax to all the preparation. Only 12 congregations joined the synod at that first meeting – less than had been involved in the previous meetings. The representatives from Michigan were late, because they had to take the long route north on Lake Huron and down Lake Michigan. The ice hadn't melted yet, so their boat was delayed.

Transportation problems kept some congregations from becoming

First St. Paul's Lutheran Church, where the first synodical convention was held, looked like this in 1847.

members at the first convention. Another factor was that the new constitution required that both the pastor and congregations become members. If one pastor served several congregations, the congregations had to join as a single parish and would receive only one lay delegate. Likewise if one congregation had several pastors, only one pastor could vote at a convention. These stipulations guaranteed an even representation of clergy and laity. Also individuals could not join the synod apart from a congregation, since the synod was a collection of congregations rather than a congregation itself.

Ten pastors joined the new synod as advisory members (no vote); their congregations still belonged to other synods or were not yet sure about joining the new group.

Not a single Perry County congregation joined, though G. H. Loeber became an advisory member. O. Fuerbringer and T. J. Brohm also were advisory members at first. Walther's congregation, Trinity of St. Louis, became a voting congregation. Another Missouri congregation, in St. Charles County, also became a voting congregation. A. F. Craemer and the Frankenmuth congregation also joined. Most of the other original members were Loehe men with congregations in Indiana and Ohio, and one in New York. Some of the original 12 had had no previous involvement with the three major groups that did the spade work to organize the synod. One of the original 12 pastors, F. W. Poeschke from Illinois, was expelled from the Synod two years

40

later—for immoral conduct. One of the 10 advisory pastors later became a Roman Catholic.

The list of those who did not join is also interesting. F. C. D. Wyneken was not present and did not become a member until the following year. Other Saxon leaders and Loehe men did not join immediately but gave the new synod full support and soon became members.

Even the host congregation, St. Paul Lutheran Church in Chicago, did not join. The congregation's pastor, C. A. Selle, became an advisory member. However, his congregation had both Lutheran and Reformed members and could not join. Later the congregation split. The pastor and four members formed a new St. Paul Lutheran congregation. The majority of the members kept the building and Reformed theology, though they were also called St. Paul Lutheran Church. Another footnote to history. The Reformed St. Paul Lutheran Church was a part of a number of denominational mergers and is now with the United Church of Christ. But it still has a strong German heritage and still has worship services in the German language. Meanwhile the Missouri Synod St. Paul Church dropped German from its worship services in the early 1950s.

Walther was elected as the first president, with Sihler as the vice-president: a balanced ticket of one Saxon and one Loehe man. It is encouraging to note how soon the division of the three groups disappeared in the synodical structure. Though they had disagreements later on, they were not divided on the basis of Saxons, Loehe men, and Franconians. A layman, Mr. F. W. Barthel, a lifelong friend of Walther's, was elected treasurer.

Like a widow and widower who marry, the newly formed synod had a ready-made family. Walther offered *Der Lutheraner* to the synod as its official publication. The offer was accepted, and Walther was named editor. A theological review committee for the publication was also appointed.

Sihler also offered the practical seminary in Fort Wayne to the synod. The seminary was started in September 1846, when 11 theological students came to the U. S. from Germany. Loehe had been training young men before sending them, but it had been decided that it would be better for them to also learn about the country in which they would work as they received a theological education. The new synod accepted Sihler's offer.

There was a problem regarding the college and seminary in Perry County. It was offered to the synod on condition that it remain in Altenburg. The convention agreed to take it only if it were moved to St. Louis. It took two years to work out a deal for the college to stay in Perry County and the seminary to move to St. Louis, where it was established on South Jefferson Avenue.

The 12-day convention ended on Thursday, May 6, with plans to hold an annual convention. The next one was to be in St. Louis, beginning on the Wednesday after Trinity Sunday.

Act II ends with the new synod under way. Now we are ready to go through the 125 years of Lutheran Church — Missouri Synod history.

V. The First 25 Years
(Or "A Funny Thing Happened on the Way to the Synodical Conference")

Our tour's next stop will be 1872. It is the year Ulysses S. Grant was elected president of the United States for the second term. It had been a difficult time for the United States. Eight presidents lived in the White House during the years from 1847 to 1872; this shows the political instability of the age. During those years the United States became a group of disunited states as they split, fought against one another in the Civil War, then reknit as a country again. Despite the split the nation grew from 29 to 37 states during that time. The first states on the West Coast: California, Oregon, and Nevada came into the Union.

The Civil War had little effect on the Missouri Synod. Many denominations were divided into northern and southern groups by the political upheavals that caused the churches to continue a theological separation for decades. Walther made a number of statements approving slavery on Biblical grounds that very few of his followers would accept today—but then he was speaking in the 1860s not the 1970s. One of the men who attended the founding convention in Chicago, Wilhelm Richmann, became a chaplain in the Civil War. Of course, there were no official Lutheran chaplains, but Richmann entered the Ohio militia and continued his pastoral work while in military service.

Great things had happened to the little band of Germans who had organized the German Evangelical Lutheran Synod of Missouri, Ohio, and Other States 25 years before. Their membership increased 58% in the first three years. During the 1850s the increase was 343%—the highest percentage of growth for any decade in their history. The growth was 154% during the 60s. In 1872 they had 415 pastors working in 26 states and 77,832 baptized members.

Walther, who was also the editor of *Der Lutheraner,* president of the seminary in St. Louis, and pastor of Trinity congregation, remained the president of the synod until 1850, when he was replaced by F. C. D. Wyneken of Baltimore, Maryland. But Walther replaced

Wyneken again in 1864, so the synod had the same president in 1872 as it had elected 25 years before.

But there had been many changes. In 1850 the pastors in the eastern part of the country complained about the long trip to the Midwest to attend the synodical convention each year. They suggested the synod be divided into districts. The synod turned down the suggestion because many feared that the formation of districts would destroy the unity of the group. But the church's rapid growth compelled the idea of geographical division to return to the agenda again and again. The constitution required that the synodical president visit each congregation annually; this was becoming an impossible task.

In 1853 the synodical convention agreed to carry out the division into four districts: Northern, Western, Eastern, and Central. Look at the map on page 44 to find what District you would have lived in then. The districts were to have conventions as the synod in their own area for two years in a row. On the third year the synod would meet as a whole. This plan of meetings, with some variations—for some reason synodwide conventions were held in 1863, 1864, and 1866 —was continued until 1965. The important part was that the districts were subdivisions of the synod, not the synod a federation of the districts. Only a synodical convention could divide districts or change congregations from one district to another. Congregations and pastors could join the synod at a district convention. Each congregation continued to send a pastoral and a lay delegate to the synodical convention until 1872, when the number became too great. Circuits, made up from about 8 to 12 congregations, were formed, so a number of congregations would send one pastor and one layman to the synodical convention. Each congregation continued its representation at district conventions.

Of course all this growing didn't happen on the synodical or district level. More people were joining the congregations, and new congregations were becoming members of the Missouri Synod. There are several factors that explain the rapid growth.

1. No special significance was placed on how many joined the new synod in 1847. Those who joined were those who happened to be present. There were many others involved in the planning, who were ready to become members. Other pastors and congregations hoped to join but wanted to wait and watch for a few years to see how things were going—a rather normal human caution.

2. Many older Lutheran congregations joined the Missouri Synod. Lutherans had been in America for hundreds of years before the

Missouri Synod made the scene. Not all of them were ignoring the Lutheran teachings as they had been accused by the Missouri Synod fathers. After the new synod got going and survived some of its own pitfalls, older established congregations joined Missouri. The oldest Lutheran congregation in the United States, St. Matthew, New York City, is a member of the 125-year-old synod, yet the congregation had been established in 1664.

3. The Saxons and the Franconians were not the only Germans who took to the boats for the new world. More German Lutherans were arriving daily. Most of them were totally unacquainted with and confused by the multidenominational religious system in America. They were willing to join any church that wasn't Roman Catholic. *Der Lutheraner* especially accused the Methodists of sheep-stealing immigrant Lutherans. In fact a large German Methodist denomination did develop in the United States. Yet many of the immigrant Lutherans found their way into the Missouri Synod and added to its growth.

The synod had also inherited a mission program—though that did nothing to add to the membership statistics. The mission colony in Frankenmuth turned its Indian mission program over to the synod. Two of the Michigan leaders became an important part of Missouri's mission endeavors. August Craemer was the first secretary of the synod's mission board, and Ferdinand Sievers was a member of the same board for 43 years. The mission to the Indians received much attention in *Der Lutheraner* and was the subject of many missionary sermons. The story of one baptism in the Indian mission was told again and again in pulpits and classrooms.

In those days there was no synodical budget, but church members gave special offerings for mission work. The work among the Indians was called heathen missions because it was proclaiming the Gospel to non-Christians. Gathering German Lutherans into the synod was called inner missions because they were already Christians.

On December 3, 1855, Lutherans in Edwardsville, Illinois, held the first recorded mission festival. The idea was suggested by two laymen who had heard of the Indian mission and wanted to help. The custom grew and soon many congregations held annual mission festivals—often in the fall when all the crops were in, and the farmers were sure how much had been given to them so they could also know how much to give. Mission festivals soon became an opportunity for social contacts among congregations, as the added attractions of dinner on the grounds and an afternoon speaker from the next circuit or from a distance were added to the program. Often mission festivals became

46

REV. E. R. BAIERLEIN   REV. J. F. BUENGER

the equivalent of a college homecoming, as former members would return for the special event. The first mission festival in English was in Baltimore in 1868.

The promotion and support of the Indian mission program was great. But there was a problem — it was difficult to keep up with the Indians and their moves. The native Americans were used to a nomadic life, and at times the government was also forcing them to move to new areas. The Indians and the Germans had totally different ideas about a colony.

The native Americans and the adopted Americans also had totally different life-styles. The Indian children didn't want to go to school all day or to memorize the Catechism. The Indians complained about long German sermons. A Leipzig missionary, Edward Baierlein, had translated the Catechism into the language of the Chippewas, and the Lutherans tried to work in the Indians' tongue, but they also expected the Indians to learn their language.

Finally the Indian mission was closed. It had to be chalked up as a failure. But as in many failures, it at least contributed to education. It was a bitter lesson for the synod, but it contributed to awareness of the need to understand the culture of people to whom one ministered. There was also a spiritual gain from the mission effort among American Indians. Today, near St. Louis, Michigan, one can walk through the cemetery of those native Americans who became Christians through the efforts of those early Lutheran missionaries.

The mission festivals continued. The offerings were sent to the Leipzig or Hermansburg mission societies in Germany. But the Missouri Synod had no "heathen mission" of its own.

The synod started with clearly defined ideas about heathen missions and inner missions. Though not as clearly spelled out, the early leaders were also aware of social ministry as an important part of the mission of the church. The best example of an effective leader in social ministry in the early days of the synod is Pastor Johann Friedrich Buenger.

Buenger was a candidate for the ministry back in Saxony and had planned to come with the first group of immigrants. When his mother was tossed into jail for refusing to tell where Walther had hidden his niece, Buenger stayed behind with her. Later they came with the Prussian group of about 100 immigrants who entered the United States via New York and arrived in Perry County just in time to see Stephan exiled.

Buenger was 29 years old in 1839. He taught school for Trinity Congregation in St. Louis and was ordained as Walther's assistant. He also became Walther's brother-in-law. His own personal grief gave him an unending interest in social ministry — five of his seven children died as infants.

Trinity Congregation started several schools in the St. Louis city area. These schools became centers around which daughter congregations were organized. Buenger became the pastor of one of the new churches, Immanuel. As a parish pastor he often spoke about the need for a Lutheran hospital. A member of his congregation, who owned a rooming house, rented two of his rooms (and gave two more) to be used as a place to treat sick people — the beginning of a social ministry of the church.

In 1864 the Lutheran Hospital Association raised $6,500 and purchased two houses to be used as a hospital. The St. Louis Lutheran Hospital continued to expand and relocated several times. Its final site (where it is now called the St. Louis Lutheran Medical Center) was in south St. Louis near where the seminary then was and the publishing house now is. (The medical center's school of nursing is now one of the top six diploma schools in the nation.)

In 1867 Buenger was also helpful in founding an orphanage at St. Paul Lutheran Church in Des Peres, about 15 miles west of Saint

Louis. The orphanage also accepted elderly people—the homeless old and young together.

Buenger's approach to social ministry had a long-range effect upon the Missouri Synod. He developed the idea of sponsoring social services outside the synodical budget and authority, yet having them publicly identified as synodically affiliated programs. His reasons for keeping the hospital and orphanage apart from synodical ownership were simple. One good reason was that the synod had no funds. There's no point in looking for watermelons in a desert. All funds donated to the synod were earmarked for a specific purpose. If there had to be a fund-raising program for a hospital or orphanage, it might better be done by a local group without going through the synod's treasury. There was no need for Lutherans in St. Louis to tell the Lutherans in Fort Wayne why they needed a Lutheran Hospital in Missouri.

The people in Indiana also needed, and later built, a hospital. Transportation and communication in the mid-1800s made it impossible for an institution to serve a large area. Finally, local people would have more interest in the continuing support of a program if they also had the responsibility of keeping it going.

Yet Buenger kept the hospital and orphanage identified with the work of the church. The supervising boards came from church members. Local congregations publicized the work of the institutions and collected funds. We will watch how this pattern of social ministry developed in the years that follow.

While still on the subject of Buenger, we must take time to mention one of his other important contributions to the synod. While he was still the assistant pastor of Trinity Congregation, he started the first known youth group in the synod. The young people organized in May 1848, when the synod was one year old. By the way, it was for men only—men, not boys, since its members were as old as 30 with none younger than 18.

The group's stated purpose was to provide help for needy ministerial students—a program that remained the chief project of synodical youth work for years. In 1851 Buenger wrote a front-page article about youth programs for *Der Lutheraner*. Trinity's program became a model for other congregations. By 1855 there were at least 23 youth societies in the synod. There was an attempt to form a federation of the youth societies, but nothing came of it.

An article about a Baltimore youth society appeared in *Der Lu-*

theraner in 1859. In addition to helping needy theological students they included in their purpose efforts to fight against a sinful world.

Ladies' groups were also concerned about seminary students. In 1852 ladies in Fort Wayne organized to sew, mend, wash, and iron for students at the practical seminary. Mrs. Walther's sewing circle began the same year in St. Louis. The sewing circle "gladdened the heart of many a student away from home through the motherly concern shown him."

During its first 25 years of history most of the congregations in the Missouri Synod operated Christian day schools. Typically these were one-room, eight-grade (or less) schools, and often they were established in communities before there were public schools. Church school teachers were among the professional church workers in the Saxon migration. Teachers had conducted classes aboard the ships as they crossed the Atlantic and started schools as soon as they arrived in Perry County. However, in most areas the pastor also taught the elementary school. By 1872 there were 472 schools — some congregations, such as those in Perry County and in Frankenmuth, had more than one school. Synod's schools had 30,320 pupils.

Remember that the seminary was moved from Perry County to St. Louis in 1849. The college department of that original school remained in Perry County. It was regarded as a teacher training program. It seems that the early Missouri Synod leaders had the idea of movable schools long before the modern concept of mobile classrooms. Watch the following school relocations carefully or you'll get lost.

As the Civil War became a threat to southern Missouri, church leaders became concerned about the students in Altenburg. (A Union army was stationed in Paitzdorf, one of the Saxon villages. Because of the military presence, the town's name was changed to Uniontown.) To remove the students from danger the college was moved in 1861 from Perry County to Fort Wayne, Indiana, to become a teachers college there. In the same year the practical seminary in Fort Wayne was moved to St. Louis and was housed in the same building that the other seminary already occupied on South Jefferson. The two schools were not merged. They merely lived together for 14 years.

These moves gave the synod three schools in two locations. In 1864 the *teacher training* part of the Fort Wayne school was moved to a new location in Addison, Illinois. The school also continued in Fort Wayne — now as a pretheological school.

There were no Sunday schools in those days. The regular Sunday morning worship included *Christenlehre* (Christian teaching), a time for the pastor to instruct the children from the Catechism and the Bible. It was also a review for the adults, who were expected to listen in.

One of the big problems in the early days of the synod (and one of the reasons listed for founding the synod) was the availability of orthodox reading materials. The immigrants had brought hymnals and catechisms with them from the old country. But that also was a problem. They left Germany to free themselves from the objectionable theology of the state church. They were well aware that some of that theology had come along with them in their books. Then there was a more practical problem: they had many different kinds of hymnals. It was common for a congregation to use three or four different books in one worship service — a little confusing to those who were trying to follow along. The different hymnals in use also delayed the synod's goal of attaining unity in forms of worship.

In November 1845 Trinity Congregation in St. Louis passed a resolution for their congregation to print their own hymnals. Walther was also, in his spare time, a musician and poet. He helped write and collect hymns. The hymnal was completed a month after the synod was organized. It contained 437 hymns, prayers, Luther's Small Catechism, the Augsburg Confession (that is, the chief statement of the Lutheran faith), the Gospel and Epistle selections for the church year, the Passion History of Christ in five parts, and Josephus' description of the destruction of Jerusalem — all within 468 pocket-size pages.

Trinity Congregation gave their hymnal to the synod in 1862. It became the authorized (German, of course) hymnal for the synod and still remains in use in places where German services are held. It was revised many times — the last time in 1917.

The synod published its first German Catechism in 1857. It remained in use for the instruction of children for the rest of that century. The Catechism was printed by a private St. Louis firm, August Wiebusch and Son, a business that had become the unofficial publishing house for the synod.

And there was a lot of printing to do. *Der Lutheraner* was expanding. At the 1851 convention the synod decided to publish a secular newspaper; the St. Louis *Volksblatt* lasted for only a few years. In 1853 they began another publication, *Lehre und Wehre* (Doctrine and Defense; though tired seminary students were known to have referred to it as Leery and Weary). The new publication was to deal with theological issues for the clergy, while *Der Lutheraner* was to become a paper for lay people.

51

In 1859 the synod made a bold step and employed its first full-time staff member, Mr. M. C. Barthel. He was the general agent for the newly appointed publication committee. Working with the Wiebusch printing company, Barthel selected material for publication and supervised distribution. Barthel's salary was $600 annually, and since this was the first attempt at having a full-time employee, there were strict rules that he could not moonlight at any other work.

There was an obvious growing need for the church body to have its own printing facilities. In 1867 Trinity Congregation moved its printing equipment to a room at the seminary—the start of a synodical printery. Louis Lange, who published the *Abendschule* (Evening School, a family magazine that continued publication in German until World War I), supervised the new printshop without salary.

Two years later a synodical convention at Fort Wayne approved the establishment of a publishing house at no cost to the synod. A company was incorporated and stock was sold at $25 a share. The stock was retired from profits, so there would be no outstanding stock and no owners. Thus Concordia Publishing House was born—a printing company of the German Evangelical Lutheran Synod of Missouri, Ohio, and Other States—under the supervision of the synod but not owned by the synod. It is a nonprofit business since all profits are donated to the synod's treasury.

In 1872 Concordia Publishing House occupied this building.

The final subject for our rapid tour through the first 25 years of synodical history is an important one — that is, the synod's struggle to establish its own theological identity and its relationship with other Lutheran groups.

Those who were in the group that might have formed the Missouri Synod had a theological split even before they were united. Another group of German immigrants, led by Pastor J. A. A. Grabau had settled in New York. Their conservative theology was close to that of the Saxons. They were a larger group, 1,000 people, with less clergy — only two pastors. Through necessity lay people began to perform many tasks that had normally been done only by ordained men in the Lutheran Church.

This worried Grabau. He wrote to the pastors involved and sent copies to Loehe and Walther regarding the correctness of such practices. Loehe agreed with Grabau and said that the office of the ministry might be endangered. Grabau immediately put limits on lay involvement in pastoral duties, including a rule that a layman could not distribute Communion.

But Walther disagreed. This was the problem at the heart of the struggles in Perry County. They had made a bishop and an ordained clergy the mark of the church, and they had had troubles. It had been a difficult experience for Walther, but he had learned his lesson well. He cautioned Grabau against defining the church on the basis of the clergy — exactly the opposite of Loehe's advice.

Grabau accepted Loehe's advice and cut off all relations with Walther. However, other Loehe men did not go along with Grabau. Grabau organized the Buffalo Synod in 1845. In 1866 a large part of the Buffalo Synod joined the Missouri Synod. In case you like to know how stories end, the Buffalo Synod continued for years but never became large. In 1930 it united with the Ohio and the Iowa synods to make the American Lutheran Church.

The Grabau incident put a strain on the relationship between Walther and Loehe. However, Walther went to Germany, and the two men met for the first time. The split was healed — but only temporarily.

The same struggle over church and ministry broke out in the Michigan colonies several years after the synod was organized. Since the debate involved Loehe men, Loehe was consulted. Again Loehe came down strong for a church structure similar to that in Germany. Men who felt a close kinship to Loehe found themselves in a bind. While they knew the theological difference was minor, they agreed on all other issues, and they admired Loehe for his work for the cause of American Lutheranism; but they felt that his position limited their work. Loehe had continued to send men to America after the synod was born. In 1848 nine Loehe pastors arrived in the United States, in 1849, 12 more, in 1850 seven more.

But the Loehe men, even the ones that had arrived recently, felt that the European pastor did not understand America. These newly arrived ministers had enough struggles of their own to adapt to the new way of life. The restrictions that Loehe put on them seemed like an added burden.

The final Loehe men for the Missouri Synod arrived in 1853. There was a struggle among the pastors in Michigan for control of congregations. Those who had remained loyal to Loehe had not joined the Missouri Synod yet anyway; so there was no actual split in membership. But there was a split among the people. The Loehe followers left Michigan to start a new mission program and a new synod in Iowa.

In 1854 the Evangelical Lutheran Synod of Iowa and Other States was organized with Loehe's support from Germany. Remember that it later became a part of the American Lutheran Church. Loehe continued his work for the cause of the Lutheran Church in the United States through the Iowa Synod. Though his final work was with another synod, Loehe is still remembered as one of the important founders of the Missouri Synod and of the practical seminary in Fort Wayne.

Meanwhile other Lutheran groups were organizing, many of them also as the result of migrations from Europe, not only from Germany but also from the Scandinavian countries. The Wisconsin Synod began shortly after Missouri. The Norwegian Synod organized in 1853 and the Augustana Lutheran Church in 1860. Many of these new groups, like the Missouri Synod, formed their own synods, because they were not theologically comfortable with the practices of the General Synod. However, as they settled down in their new country, they recognized the need to work together in the general interest of Lutheranism.

In 1867 several synods withdrew from the General Synod in protest against certain practices and the lack of a theological position. Together with some independent synods they united to form a federation called the General Council. The General Council was more concerned about doctrine and the Lutheran Confessions than the General Synod of that time. The Missouri Synod did not participate in the General Council, because it did not feel a theological kinship with the member synods. The Wisconsin Synod joined the Council but was the first to withdraw.

That left the United States with two major federations of the numerous Lutheran groups. The General Synod, including more of the older Lutheran groups in the country, is the ancestor, broadly speaking of the present-day Lutheran Church in America. The General Council, including various cultural and nationality groups that had arrived later from Europe divided several times. Some of the descendants of the synods of the General Council are now in the LCA and others are in the American Lutheran Church. Please note that the eventual union of the small synods into the LCA and the ALC did not always follow the lines of the original federations of the General Synod and the General Council. Many groups switched back and forth, and others split between the two.

And some groups were not involved in either. In 1870 the Eastern District of the Ohio Synod suggested that their synod and the Missouri Synod establish a conference for conservative Lutherans. Missouri responded favorably, and a series of meetings were held. Other groups were also invited to participate.

In July 1872 the Evangelical Lutheran Synodical Conference was organized in Milwaukee. In addition to the Missouri and Ohio Synods, the Wisconsin, Norwegian, Minnesota, and Illinois Synods also joined the conference. Walther became its first president.

The Missouri Synod also became involved with another group of Lutherans in 1872 that was to have a long-range influence in the church's history. A small group of English speaking Lutherans, originally members of the Tennessee Synod (in the General Synod South), worked together in southeast Missouri, near Perry County geographically and close to the Missouri Synod theologically.

This group wanted to join the Missouri Synod, but they spoke only English. Walther attended their conference in Gravelton, Missouri, in the summer of 1872. Through an interpreter he preached to them from a wagon and encouraged them to organize their own group which would be in fellowship with the Missouri Synod. The English speaking Lutherans accepted Walther's suggestion and formed the English Evangelical Lutheran Conference of Missouri. They also started a college in Gravelton and became a moving force for English speaking conservative Lutherans.

While on the subject of language, we should be reminded of a few things about the German-English struggle in the Missouri Synod, because it becomes a major issue later on. The founders of the Missouri Synod did not want to use English as the official language of their theology. Both Loehe men and Saxons had been disappointed to find the laxity of doctrine among American Lutherans. Rightly or wrongly, they felt that the early Lutherans in the United States lost their orthodox theology because they gave up the German language. To them the English language sounded less precise than their own. They were sure of what they were communicating in German, but in English they could not find the exact words.

Insistence on the use of the German language became a big cross for Missouri Synod to bear later on, but it may have helped the synod get established on a solid footing. It is unfair to say that the founders of the synod were afraid of change. They accepted more change in their lifetime than most people. They left one country and adopted another; they struggled to hold on to their theology and yet put it in a whole new church structure.

The early synodical leaders were also willing and eager to use any language to share the Gospel. They attempted to use the Chippewa language to convert the Indians. They started a mission for Chinese people in St. Louis and used the Chinese language. And they used English for some teaching and preaching. They were willing to share the Gospel in English. But they wanted to defend it in German.

That brings us to 1872. The Missouri Synod is on its way, a quarter of a century old. Many of the original leaders are still on the scene, but there are also new faces.

VI. Getting Involved
(Or "They'll Never Believe This Back in the Old Country")

Next stop is in 1897, the 50th anniversary of the German Evangelical Lutheran Synod of Missouri, Ohio, and Other States. William McKinley became the president of the United States in 1897 — and there were 45 states by then. He had defeated William J. Bryan the year before. Bryan's campaign has been based on "free silver," and McKinley's on "sound money." Because the nation was again recovering from a financial crisis, the issue of money was important. The Gold Standard Act was adopted 3 years later. The year after McKinley came into office the Spanish-American War started — and ended.

Much had happened in the Missouri Synod in its second 25 years of history. During the 1870s membership had increased by 90%. During the next 10 years the growth was 332%; in the 1890s the increase was 39%. At the end of the first 50 years the Missouri Synod had 687,334 baptized members in 1,986 congregations and 683 preaching stations. There were 1,565 men on the clergy roster.

New synodical districts had been added. Find your home on the map (p. 58), and you will see what district you would have belonged to in 1897. Also notice that one of the original four districts has been divided up — the Northern District was the first of the original four to be replaced by all new districts.

At the 1878 convention Walther asked to be relieved as synodical president. He had held the office for a total of 19 years along with numerous other duties. The convention heeded Walther's request and elected in his place the Rev. H. C. Schwan. The new president was F. C. D. Wyneken's nephew, his sister's son. Schwan added another dimension to the president's office in that when he had migrated from Europe he went to Brazil rather than to the United States. Six years later, at Wyneken's invitation, he came to the United States and served a congregation in Missouri for two years and then took a call to Ohio. He later was elected president of the Central District.

Schwan also was the first synodical president to serve the synod full time. Even with the division into districts the growth in the number of congregations in the synod placed a heavy load on its president. Yet there was a strong feeling that every ordained minister should be a parish pastor or a missionary assigned to the specific task of teaching the Gospel. Remember that the only full-time staff person, the general manager of the publishing house, was not ordained. Professors of synodical schools also served as assistant pastors in nearby congregations to keep their identity as being part of the parish ministry.

Nevertheless the Fort Wayne convention in 1881 made Schwan a full-time president. There were no synodical offices in those days. He continued as an associate pastor in Ohio, but no congregational duties were allowed to interfere with his primary work as president of the synod.

The second 25 years of Missouri Synod history continued one doctrinal struggle and started another. First, the continuation of theological struggles — this time the chiliastic and predestinarian controversies. Second, the development and expansion of new ministries.

We lead off with chiliasm — the problem wasn't how to pronounce it or how to spell the word — it's a doctrine which says that Christ will rule on earth for a thousand years. The problem was that millennialism

REV. H. C. SCHWAN
PRESIDENT, 1878 – 1899

(another word for the thousand-year rule) got involved. Some were premillenialists, who believed that Christ would judge the world and then establish a kingdom here that would last for a thousand years. Others were post-millennialists, who taught that Christ would come, operate a kingdom on earth for a thousand years, then schedule Judgment Day. It seems like a minor point to argue about since the doctrine would have little to do with our life now or in eternity, because Christ is the one who makes the arrangements. But those who got involved in millennialism thought it was very important, and it distracted from many other important teachings.

Millennialism had never been an issue in the Lutheran Church. It was generally connected with Fundamentalist groups. However, in the spirit of revivalism that swept the country after the Civil War, millennialism got into several Lutheran synods.

It hit the Missouri Synod through G. A. Schieferdecker, one of the original Saxons and the first president of the Western District. Schieferdecker was pastor of Trinity Congregation in Altenburg, Perry County. His views on millennialism caused a rift between himself and the other leaders of the Missouri Synod. Not only were the problems of pre- and post-millennialism discussed but also whether the doctrine was an "open question," that is, could there be different views accepted? Walther and others refused to treat the matter as an open question. There was no room for any teaching that gave Christ a literal earthly kingdom for a thousand years.

Schieferdecker was expelled from the Missouri Synod, along with a small segment of his congregation. He joined the Iowa Synod and began a second congregation in Altenburg. Later Schieferdecker returned to the Missouri Synod, but the second congregation remained a part of the Iowa Synod. Through two mergers the congregation became a part of the American Lutheran Church that declared altar and pulpit fellowship with Missouri in 1969. After over a hundred years of separation the two congregations in Altenburg now exchange pastors for Lenten services and in other ways live out the fellowship officially declared by their church bodies.

The chiliastic controversy was a minor tremor compared to the quake that followed in the predestinarian controversy. It affected not only the Missouri Synod but the entire Synodical Conference.

For the first few years the synods of the Synodical Conference had lived in harmony. The Ohio Synod gave Walther the doctor of divinity title in 1878. The St. Louis seminary called a member of the Ohio Synod to its chair of English theology. Though the call was not accepted, it showed the close relationship that existed for a while. It looked as though the Synodical Conference would become a unifying force for conservative Lutheranism in America.

But the dreams of a solid front of orthodox Lutherans were destroyed by the predestinarian controversy. Though this is a brief history book, we'll have to take the time to study a little theology in order to follow the problems of the Synodical Conference.

The big thing about theology for all Lutherans is that it keeps everything centered in Jesus Christ. They may approach subjects from different points of view and use different words, but it has to come out that God does His thing for us through Christ and that Christ is our way to reunion with God. Because the doctrine of Christ starts as God's action toward man (when Christ became a human being with us) and then faces the issues of life, death, and life again; it makes everything about Christianity depend upon God's action and God's motives, not man's action or man's motives. We don't earn, deserve, or help receive our salvation. It is, in Reformation talk, by grace through faith in Christ alone.

Any time that Christianity is presented in these simple terms as being God's action, someone is sure to ask, "Then why are some saved and not others?" The question is so simple (even Sunday school children ask it) and yet so difficult to answer that it is embarrassing to some theologians. To make the question seem more worthy of discussion it is often asked in Latin, *cur alii prae aliis:* why some and not others? Some take the easy way and ignore the question. But that can be dangerous too. By working out his own theology, each individual ends up finding some system by which he saves, or at least helps save, himself. That is dead-end thinking because Christ has already done it for us in that we can't do it ourselves.

Some answer "Why some and not others?" by saying that people are different. Some do more good, or less evil, or try harder, and the like. Those answers forget the fact that we are all sinners and that any sin puts us all in the same bag—eternal death. The other possible answer to the question seems to be that God chooses some and not others. That's where predestination comes in.

The Reformed churches, especially those heavy on Calvinism, taught a strong form of predestination that said God had chosen some for heaven and He had chosen some for hell. That doctrine was one reason why the Lutherans in Germany objected to any merger with Reformed churches.

But that still leaves the Lutherans with an unanswered question.

Just why is it that anyone can go to hell when Jesus died for all people and God wants all people to be saved? Some answers given were:

1. Because some believe and some don't—the danger of that as it stands is that it sounds as though believing becomes the one good work that saves. "Because I believe, I am saved," puts the action on man. But Lutheran theology says that even faith is a gift of God. By grace God gives us faith.

2. Because some resist God's grace more than others. That answer has problems too. It makes some less hardhearted than others and thereby they contribute to their salvation by not being as bad as others. It won't preach.

3. Another answer, one that some Lutherans held, is that God used His foreknowledge to look ahead and see who would believe and He then predestined them to believe. But that makes God's action based on man's again. If God looked ahead and saw faith and then rewarded it, salvation is not by grace alone.

Conservative Lutherans (and some others too, since that is not the major issue between the groups) wanted to make sure that they taught a way of salvation that depended 100% on Christ and 0% on man. So the way one answered the question, "Why some and not others?" became the way to make the true Lutherans stand out.

There had always been some tension between the Missouri and Ohio Synods on the subject of predestination. (By the way, things had happened to the Ohio Synod in the last 25 years, too. Remember that the Loehe men pulled out because they thought the Ohio Synod was getting too English and too liberal. Later many English congregations left the same synod, because they thought it was staying too German and too conservative. This did make the Ohio Synod more conservative, and the Loehe men found their original fellowship with that group reestablished in the Synodical Conference.)

As early as 1872 an Ohio Synod pastor had called Walther a "crypto-Calvinist," that is a hidden Calvinist: one who taught that God predestined salvation by looking ahead for faith but who wouldn't admit that he was teaching Calvinism. Walther defended himself with the aid of fellow seminary faculty members, including F. A. Schmidt. Schmidt was from St. Louis and had been confirmed by Walther. In 1876 Schmidt transferred to the Norwegian seminary, which meant that he left Missouri. But there was no doctrinal problem. There was a close relationship between the two synods. Schmidt even later indicated a willingness to return to the St. Louis seminary. The debate between Walther and the Ohio Synod man was cleared up—at least on the surface.

Walther presented a number of essays to the Western District conventions on the general subject that all glory and credit for salvation must be given to God alone. At the Altenburg convention in 1877 Walther's theme was: "The Lutheran Church teaches that it is false and wrong to teach that not the mercy of God and the most holy merit of Christ alone, but that also in us there is a cause of the election of God, for the sake of which God has elected us unto eternal life." Which being interpreted is, "God didn't save us because He saw anything good in us." The big thrust of the paper was against the third answer above to the question "why some and not others?" The essay was printed and distributed.

On January 2, 1879, Prof. Schmidt notified Walther that he disagreed with the essay and told President Schwan that he intended to make his complaints public unless they were handled promptly. (Members of the Synodical Conference had an agreement not to air theological differences in public print without first attempting to work them out.)

Unfortunately the president of the Synodical Conference at that time was seriously ill and could not call a special meeting to discuss the issue. Schmidt believed that his complaint was being ignored, so he published an attack against Walther. Missouri Synod pastoral conferences in some areas jumped in to defend Walther. Other Missourians disagreed with Walther. Most Ohio Synod pastors backed Schmidt.

The president of the Synodical Conference died, and the new president called a meeting for January 5, 1881, 2 years after the initial complaint. By then most minds were made up. The Ohio Synod delegates left after 5 days. Walther was angered because he had been called a Calvinist. From his point of view the Ohio Synod had always had a touch of Calvinism on the subject of predestination.

(By the way, to answer that question, "Why some and not others?" Walther did not answer it, but he did not ignore it. The Scripture says if man is lost it is his fault. If man is saved it is to God's credit. To go beyond Scripture and give a final answer denies one or the other. On subjects where the Scripture is silent, man should be silent too.)

At the May 1881 convention the Missouri Synod convention adopted a 13-point statement regarding predestination. There was lengthy debate, but a position backing Walther was accepted. After the convention, a group of Missouri Synod pastors left the synod to organize the Evangelical Lutheran Conference, which joined the Ohio Synod in 1882. After the Ohio Synod convention, in September 1881, a group of their pastors withdrew to form the Concordia Synod of Pennsylvania and Other States, which later became a part of the Missouri Synod.

The controversy divided families and lifelong friends. It spread into all the synods of the Synodical Conference. The Ohio Synod withdrew from the conference in protest against Missouri. The Norwegian Synod, to which Schmidt belonged, was divided. It withdrew from the Synodical Conference, not in protest but to try to handle the issue alone. Feelings were so strong that the Norwegians split into two and then three groups. The third group was called the Anti-Missouri Synod Brotherhood. It continued until 1890, when it merged with another Norwegian group.

The controversy had shuffled pastors and congregations among the synods of the Synodical Conference. But it was the Synodical Conference that suffered more than the individual synods, except maybe for the Norwegian. Though the conservative conference continued with six member synods, it did not regain the unity that it had had before.

Despite the theological controversy of the 1880s that decade gave the Missouri Synod the second highest percentage of membership growth of any 10-year period in its history. The controversy did not cause the growth. Many other things were happening at the same time. We now turn our attention to the more important development of the Synod's second quarter—the development of new ministries.

First let's look at what happened to the mission program.

Missouri Synod's first overseas missionary (though they would never have dreamed of calling him that) was Pastor H. Ruhland who accepted a call away from his congregation in Pleasant Ridge, Illinois, to serve a congregation in Dresden, Saxony, in April 1872.

Walther had kept track of the folks "back home." He visited Germany again in 1860. The Germans also kept up on their American friends via *Der Lutheraner*. Other pastors in Saxony had continued to oppose the state church. Some left it and started a free church—no government connections. They asked Walther to recommend a pastor and Ruhland was suggested.

Other Missouri Synod pastors also went to Europe to free-church congregations. Though this was never a part of an official mission program, it was the first successful assist given to other Christians beyond the synodical boundaries.

But the major mission work among Germans was done in the United States. Walther's son-in-law, Stephanus Keyl, made a trip to Europe to establish a method of contacting German Lutherans before they left for the New World. This early idea of a referral system would have made it easier for pastors in America to minister to arriving Lutherans. However, the Lutheran state churches in Europe had little interest in referring anyone to the Missouri Synod.

Therefore Keyl in 1869 started a Lutheran Pilgrim House in New York City, where he worked for 36 years. He would meet incoming ships and help the immigrants. Those who spoke only German were especially in need of Keyl's ministry. Through his efforts many Germans came into a favorable contact with the Missouri Synod. Keyl was also the first Missouri Synod pastor to make wide use of tracts printed in many languages. A similar ministry was established in Baltimore in 1872. The coming of Germans to the United States reached its peak in the 1880s—the big reason for the Missouri Synod's rapid growth at that time.

Not all immigrants were contacted when they got off the boat. Those who were needed a follow-up ministry when they arrived at their permanent homes in the Midwest. There were not enough pastors to keep up with the influx of new people.

Colporteurs (book salesmen) became an important part of the church's ministry. These men traveled throughout the country, selling Bibles, hymnals, catechisms, and other religious publications. They provided devotional material for families and small unorganized groups of Lutherans. They would also locate Lutheran families and arrange for pastors to make contact, when there were special needs such as baptism and confirmation instruction. Colporteurs often had the status of circuit riding ministers among the people; they provided an important ministry.

After the mission to the Indians closed down, most Missouri Synod mission money was sent to the Leipzig or Hermannsburg mission societies in Germany. These societies were not a part of the state church but were independent mission groups often supported financially by members of the state churches. Through these societies the Missouri Synod still was involved in "heathen" mission work, because the societies had missionaries in India.

But that arrangement came to a screeching halt by 1876. Four missionaries in India accused the mission societies of allowing false doctrine. These missionaries used Walther and the Missouri Synod to support their charges. All four left the mission field. Two returned to

Germany and two, Carl [Manthey] Zorn and Fritz [John Frederick] Zucker, came to America and were accepted as Missouri Synod pastors. In 1872 97 congregations of the Missouri Synod sent money to the Hermannsburg society and 53 to the Leipzig society. In 1876 the score was zero for both.

What an embarrassing position for the Missouri Synod! It had a mission board. No one wanted to give up the annual mission festivals raising money for missions. *Der Lutheraner* had done a good job in stressing the importance of "heathen missions." But there was no mission program.

Working through the Synodical Conference, the synod explored the possibilities of starting mission work among the black people of the South. Interestingly, this was regarded as "heathen" missions rather than "inner" missions even though the great majority of black people in the United States were nominally Christian.

There were several unsuccessful attempts to start Lutheran congregations in black communities in the South. The first missionary sent recognized the need for a new approach. Receiving little help and much opposition from white Lutherans in the area, he worked closely with other Protestant denominations—a practice that caused him problems with Synodical Conference leaders.

When Friedrich Berg graduated in 1878 from the St. Louis seminary he went to Arkansas to work with black people. To his Missouri Synod friends it must have appeared that Berg was going all the way in his effort to communicate. He did his evangelizing in English. But to the black people of Arkansas in 1878 he might as well have been speaking German. He attempted to follow not only established Lutheran doctrine but also established Lutheran practices. The lesson of the failure of the Indian mission had not been digested yet. Berg's efforts to explain infant baptism, conduct liturgical services, and have weekly confirmation classes with memory work amazed the people with whom he worked. His frustration and determination typifies that of the Synod as it struggled to do what it knew should be done in missions and yet follow the strict patterns it had set for itself.

After 3 years Berg took a call to Indiana. But his story should be finished—30 years later he went back to work among black people as a teacher and as president of Immanuel College in Greensboro, North Carolina.

Pastor Nils J. Bakke finally provided the continued leadership that got the Lutheran Church started among black people in the South. Bakke was a German-speaking Norwegian who came to the St. Louis seminary from nonsynodical schools—an unusual accomplishment in those days. But later he did marry a lady named Concordia. He had the right blend of sound Lutheran doctrine and an understanding of the special social needs in the area where he worked. Bakke arrived in New Orleans in 1880. His work was difficult and with limited success. We'll hear more about him in the next chapter, which means he made it.

As another "heathen" mission project the synod sent a Jewish Lutheran, Daniel Landsmann, to work among Jewish people in New York in 1881. Though Landsmann had attended the Springfield seminary he was never ordained. He worked as an evangelist in a lonely and difficult area for years. Perhaps his greatest success was that a young man who became a Christian through his efforts succeeded him in his ministry.

The first Missouri Synod congregation in Canada was established in 1879. The church expanded rapidly there, also primarily through migration, so that as the synod celebrated its 50th birthday there was a separate Canadian district with 42 congregations. Ernst, one of the original Loehe men, was the first district president.

The synod also continued to expand its mission in social ministry during its second quarter. The pattern established by J. F. Buenger continued. Orphanages were started in Addision, Illinois, in 1873, and in New Orleans in 1881. Lutherans in Detroit also planned to start an orphanage and called Pastor George Speckhard to be its superintendent. Speckhard hesitated to accept the call because he was preparing two deaf girls for confirmation. But he took the call and brought the girls along. Because of Speckhard's interest and ability in the education of deaf children, the Detroit institution became a school for the deaf rather than an orphanage.

Youth work also progressed. There was an effort to establish an association of youth groups from all Lutheran synods, but it failed. Finally, on May 23, 1893, 16 delegates from 12 societies met at Trinity Lutheran Church in Buffalo, New York, and organized the first continuing youth program in the synod. The following year the organization met in Fort Wayne and called themselves the *Walther-Liga* (Walther League). They were still a male-only organization.

The 1872 to 1907 span of Missouri Synod history also included new developments in education.

The two seminaries continued to operate at one address in Saint Louis. Each continued its original purpose. The one that had started in Fort Wayne was the practical seminary requiring less academic background and less study of classical languages. The seminary that had begun in Perry County still provided a classical European education.

The building that housed the two schools was overcrowded. There was talk of merging the schools or discontinuing the practical seminary.

The problem was solved by a chain of events that started in 1852 when the Synod of North Illinois established Illinois State University (Abraham Lincoln took his only college courses there) in Springfield, Illinois. In 1870 the Pennsylvania Ministerium bought the school for use as an orphanage. Their plans didn't work out, so they offered the land to the Missouri Synod. Buenger had long wanted the synod to start a college for girls. He followed his well-tested pattern and asked Trinity Congregation in Springfield to buy the land for a future college.

But when the Synod at their 1874 convention voted to keep the practical seminary, they had to find a new place to put it. The Springfield site was chosen. In 1875 the school moved to Springfield, where it is today. Of the 113 students enrolled during its first year in Springfield, only 53 were Missouri Synod. Other students came from the Wisconsin and Norwegian Synods and 33 were from Germany. And two students were members of the English Conference.

Meanwhile the St. Louis seminary continued to expand, and again facilities were overcrowded. In 1883 new buildings were constructed on the same location in south St. Louis.

A number of new schools (now junior colleges), then called preparatory schools, opened during the latter part of the 19th century. In 1881 Concordia College in Milwaukee, Wisconsin, was opened by the Northwestern and Illinois Districts. They gave the school to the synod in 1887. Also in 1881 the New York pastoral conference asked St. Matthew Congregation in New York City to open an academy. The school was given to the Eastern District in 1882. It was moved to Hawthorne [Neperan], New York, in 1894. The Eastern District in turn gave it to the synod in 1896. Another Concordia College was begun in New Orleans in 1881, but it closed in 1887.

In 1883 St. Paul College was begun in Concordia, Missouri. As an interesting twist, about 10 years later a Concordia College was founded in St. Paul, Minnesota.

People in the western part of the synod felt that the church needed another college to train Christian day school teachers. In 1894 such a college was opened in Seward, Nebraska.

Another far-reaching development in education occurred in 1884 when 13 women started teaching in Lutheran day schools. None of them were trained in the synodical system, since female students were not accepted. Yet those women opened the doors for a new vocation in teaching for many Christian women.

Synod's publishing facilities also continued to expand. Concordia Publishing House built a new plant in 1874. The plant has been expanded several times but has remained in the same area to this day. The synod printed its own textbooks for the parochial schools. Their report for 1890 shows they produced in that year: hymn books, 45,000; catechisms, 25,000; readers, 19,000; English readers, 25,000; Bibles, 6,000. In 1879 the publishing house printed the first of a 25-volume set of Luther's writings. The set, called the "St. Louis Edition," was completed in 1910.

A scandal hit the synod in 1891. The general manager of the publishing house, M. C. Barthel, was accused of having stolen money from the business. The Barthel family replaced all the money that had been stolen. Barthel was replaced by Martin S. Tirmenstein.

That small group of English speaking Lutherans that started in 1872 continued to grow and continued to try to get into the Missouri Synod. They finally formed their own synod but were refused membership in the Synodical Conference (on the grounds they should join the Missouri Synod) until 1890. The English Synod also had a strong interest in education. In 1893 they accepted Concordia College in Conover, North Carolina. It was closed in 1935. In 1893 St. John's College in Winfield Kansas, became an English Synod project. It is still in operation today.

In 1882 the Cleveland pastoral conference of the English Synod of Missouri and Other States published the first issue of the *Lutheran Witness*, Pastor C. A. Frank, editor. The paper soon became the official paper of the English Synod. In those days the list of new subscribers was published in each issue. It also offered news and editorials on the issues of the day. One editorial speaks against birth control and calls such practices murder. Another criticized a minister of another denomination because he refused to preach in a worship service because a black man was present.

But the chief function of the *Lutheran Witness* was to present Missouri Synod's views to the English speaking world. Though the English Synod was not at the time in the Missouri structure, its sympathies were. During all the theological controversies other Lutheran papers printed strong attacks against Missouri. And *Der Lutheraner* printed equally strong attacks against the others. The problem was that many in the other synods couldn't read German. The *Lutheran Witness* got the word out in a language that could be understood.

First Number of the Lutheran Witness presented this appearance.

One of the gradual steps toward the use of the English language occurred in 1890. At the synodical convention in Milwaukee Prof. F. Pieper of the St. Louis seminary encouraged the use of some English at synodical schools so the pastors would be able to preach respectable English if the need arose. He assured the delegates that it would not destroy the doctrine of the Missouri Synod or lead to such excesses as the ordination of women. The suggestion was given a "ja" vote.

Because some of the tensions between the Missouri Synod and other Lutherans have been mentioned, don't think that all other Lutherans were against the group they generally called "German Lutherans." It's just that tensions often make history. In 1889 the *Lutheran Observer,* published for the General Synod, told its readers that in a short time the Missouri Synod had become the largest *general body* (meaning the synods themselves, not federations) of Lutherans in the United States. The editorial gave Missouri Synod's faithfulness to the Scripture and the Lutheran Confessions and its unity among its members as the reasons for the rapid growth.

By the time the Missouri Synod celebrated its 50th anniversary most of the original cast of characters were gone. G. H. Loeber had been the first of the charter members to die. His death was in 1849, two years after the synod was founded.

F. C. D. Wyneken died in May 1876 in San Francisco, California, an unusual place for a pastor president of the Missouri Synod in those days, but Wyneken had stayed true to form as a man to do new things.

J. F. Buenger died in 1882. Also true to form until the last, Buenger was planning another social ministry, a mental asylum, when he was taken by death. Dr. Wilhelm Sihler died in 1885.

Dr. C. F. W. Walther died in St. Louis, while the 1887 synodical convention was being held in Fort Wayne. He was 75 years old and had celebrated the 50th anniversary of his ordination.

August F. Craemer had asked to retire in 1875, when the practical seminary (he was on the faculty) moved to Springfield. He was also serving a congregation that he had founded in St. Louis and preferred to stay there. He was also having health problems again. But the synod asked him to stay with the seminary, and he did. He also became the pastor of a congregation near Springfield, where he carried on until he died in April 1891.

Ottomar Fuerbringer died in 1892 and J. A. Ernst in 1895. These men lived to see the little synod they had founded in Chicago grow beyond their wildest dreams. How often they must have thought "They'll never believe this back in the old country."

VII. A German Synod Goes International
(Or "Hey, There's an English Word for 'Jesus'")

Now by the miracle of author's privilege we jump to 1922. Warren Harding, the man who "looked like a president," lived in the White House. The nation had 48 states, and most people thought the flag would forever have 48 stars. World War I, the war to end all wars, was over. The League of Nations had been established and turned down by the U. S. Senate. The postwar period was a gutsy time to live in the United States and Canada. A great future appeared to be just over the horizon. The financial picture was bright, employment high, and politics stable.

And the Missouri Synod was 75 years old. Its membership had gone over one million: 1,041, 514 baptized members to be exact. That was a 20% increase for the first 10 years of the century and another 14% from 1910 to 1920, the lowest percentage of increase per decade in the synod's history. There were 2,669 congregations and preaching stations with 3,073 pastors—including those in special ministries and those retired. There were Missouri Synod congregations in every state except Arizona, Georgia, and South Carolina. The synod had also expanded in Canada with congregations in Quebec and British Columbia. There were three Canadian districts.

Three men served as president of the synod during its third quarter of a century. Schwan continued until 1899, when he asked not to be renominated. Francis Pieper, who like Walther was the president of Concordia Seminary, St. Louis, was elected in his place. He did not resign from his seminary position, so the synod again had a part-time president. But not for long. The load of the double presidency caused Dr. Pieper to suffer some severe health problems, and he had to choose between one or the other. At the 1911 synodical convention he asked to be relieved of his duties as president of the synod. Frederick Pfotenhauer became the fourth president and again the office was full-time. Pfotenhauer established an office in Chicago.

During this span of history a more centralized synodical organization began to develop. In 1905 the synod appointed a General Board

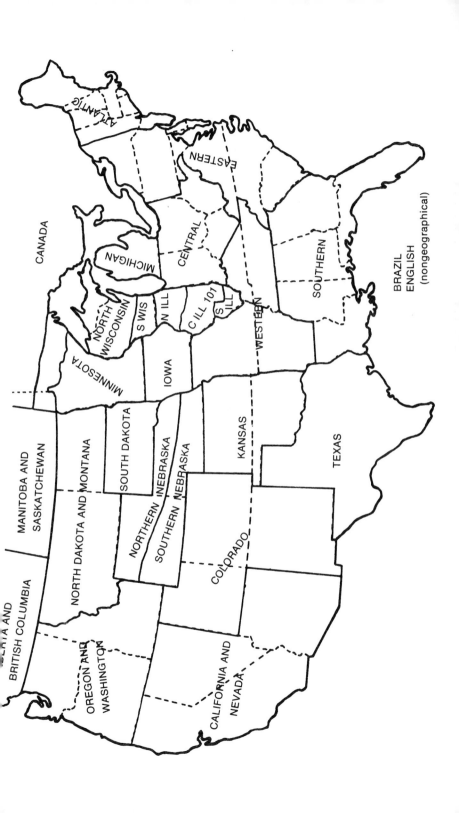

DR. F. PIEPER   **DR. F. PFOTENHAUER**

of Supervision for the educational institutions. In 1917 the Board of Supervision was replaced with a Board of Directors, a supervising body for the entire synodical structure. The numerous boards and committees that had gradually developed within the synod were one-by-one organized into departments under the Board of Directors.

As the missions and ministries of the synod expanded, its method of financial support became a nightmare. Each program continued to plug its own cause. Gifts to synod were being earmarked for a specific task that the donor wanted to support. Financial reports included page after page of dollar and cent contributions. Each program of the church also had to use its own manpower to beat the drums for more financial support. Not only was this a duplication of effort, but it also caused an unhealthy competition among various mission efforts.

To relieve the program people were encouraged to give offerings to the "general synod," undesignated funds that would be divided among synodical projects according to needs. In the early part of the 1900s double-pocket offering envelopes were introduced. Offerings placed on the "home" side went to the congregation's treasury. Offerings on the other side, "missions," went to districts and synod. These offering envelopes were sometimes given free to congregations to introduce more church members to the idea of supporting synod through regular offerings instead of only through a once-a-year mission festival for a specific project.

Another change made by a synodical convention seems small, but it is symbolic of the development of the synod during the first third of the 20th century. Meeting in Milwaukee in 1917, the synod dropped the word German from its official title and became, "The Evangelical Lutheran Synod of Missouri, Ohio, and Other States."

Considering the fact that the United States declared war on Germany in 1917, the deletion of "German" from the letterhead seems to have a simple explanation. As the usual characterizations of the "enemy" became a part of the American way of thinking about the new German nation, the old German culture, now two and three generations away from German citizenship, became suspect. Lutheran schools were forbidden to teach the German language. People who spoke German in their homes were looked upon as disloyal citizens. There was nothing else to do but say, "Ich bin ein Amerikaner."

But the official change of the synodical name indicates much more than a reaction to World War I. Perhaps it took the war to help make the church aware of the fact, but their name was misleading. They were no longer a German church.

A number of changes had occurred during the early part of the 1900s that had a great influence on the future direction of the Missouri Synod. Let's look at the more important ones.

First, the synod finally got a true foreign mission program started. The first overseas mission field was opened at the tail end of the previous quarter, but it took a while for the mission to develop.

Early in 1894 two more missionaries to India, who had been sponsored by German mission societies, objected to the theological practices of their fellow missionaries. Theodore [K. G. T.] Naether and Francis Mohn appealed to the Missouri Synod for theological support. However, rather than repeat the previous experience of changing overseas missionaries to Missouri Synod pastors working in the United States, the newly appointed Board for World Missions (established on May 6, 1893) encouraged the missionaries to continue to work in India. Naether and Mohn were accepted into the Missouri Synod and commissioned as missionaries to India on October 14, 1894.

So the Missouri Synod entered its third quarter with two overseas missionaries. At the end of that quarter there were 27 missionaries — 21 working as evangelists, two as teachers, and four in medical missions. The mission field was also served by 225 local helpers.

Though the world mission program started as a one-way street, that is, the American Christians had a message to give to people in less fortunate circumstances, the success of that message eventually gave the Missouri Synod a response from the mission fields beyond the statistics of the number of people baptized. The cumulative lessons of the early work among American Indians, the Southern blacks, and now overseas areas had an influence on the synod. Missionaries struggled under the load of maintaining not only the true doctrine but also a way to live out that doctrine in one culture while trying to satisfy the demands of another culture back home. Missionary reports, families home on furlough, and missionaries who returned to serve congregations in the United States all contributed to the development of a wider view of the church in ministry.

The mission work in India grew. A second field was opened. The synod entered the field of medical missions in 1913 by sending nurses to work with the missionaries. In 1921 Dr. Theodore Doederlein, a Chicago physician, volunteered to go to India for several years to help establish a hospital.

The interest in overseas missions grew. Prof. Edward L. Arndt of St. Paul, Minnesota, graduate of the St. Louis seminary and professor at the St. Paul Concordia, resigned as a teacher in 1910 to promote Lutheran mission work in China. He organized the Evangelical Lu-

REV. E. L. ARNDT

76

theran Mission for China in May 1912—following the European example of a mission society outside the church structure. The next year Arndt became the organization's first missionary to go to China. Within 4 years two more missionaries had joined him, and Lutheran congregations were established. In 1917 the Evangelical Lutheran Mission for China asked the synod to take over its work. The synod accepted the offer, and the attempt at extracurricular mission societies was dropped. By 1922 the China mission program had 381 baptized members and operated schools for 1,073 students. That year they also established a seminary.

Synod's foreign mission program finally had a taste of success. Again the official publications and the mission festival sermons could share the excitement of people involved in Christ's mission command to go out to the world.

But the world was also still coming to the United States. The continued migration from countries other than Germany provided another reason to drop the name German from the synod's official title.

The synodical convention of 1899 in St. Louis appointed a Board for Foreign Tongue Missions. The new board was not involved in overseas missions but in "inner" missions. The delegates had faced the fact that it was not enough to use English in addition to German. Other languages were needed as well.

Mission work among Lutheran Estonians had begun in 1892 and became a part of the synodical program in 1899. Work with Lithuanians was made a part of the synod in 1908. By 1922 four pastors served eight Lithuanian congregations. Work among the Polish Lutherans began in 1908. In 1911 the Foreign Tongue Mission Board started a mission congregation for Lutheran Finns.

Not all the foreign tongue mission work was with immigrants from Lutheran countries. For about 10 years there was an effort to do mission work among Persian immigrants. Though the effort reached many people for a while, it dwindled and was discontinued by 1920. A former Roman Catholic priest had become a Lutheran and opened a mission among Italians in New Jersey. In 1916 he became a Missouri Synod pastor and gave his mission station to the synod. By 1922 it had 92 baptized members.

Another immigrant Lutheran group that was to have a lasting relationship with the Missouri Synod appeared during this time. Slovak Lutherans began making plans to form their own synod as far back as 1894. They published their own periodical, *Church Leaves*. The Slovak Evangelical Lutheran Synod of the U. S. A. organized at a series of pastoral conferences in Pennsylvania from 1899 to 1902. The synod's doctrine and practice was close to Missouri, and it joined the Synodical Conference.

Strangely enough, the Missouri Synod also found a new mission field among American Indians. A group of descendants of the Mohicans had settled near Shawano, Wisconsin. The Presbyterian Church had initiated mission work among them but could not continue it. They asked a Missouri Synod pastor, Theodore Nickel, to continue the work. Pastor Nickel assumed responsibility for the mission program in 1898 and gave it to the synod the following year. A school was established, and several more congregations were begun. This time the work continued.

Even the Missouri Synod's connections in Europe lost the "German Club" appearance. Though the war disrupted relationships with Missouri for a short time, the Saxon Free Church continued to grow. In 1911 the Free Church of Denmark united with the Saxon Free Church. The same year two congregations in London, England, became members of the Missouri Synod as a part of the Atlantic District. Fellowship ties were also established with the Lutheran Church in Australia and New Zealand.

Many European Lutherans had also migrated to South America. Their struggles to establish a church were similar to those of the Missourians in North America. In 1900 the Missouri Synod answered a request of Lutherans in Brazil to send a pastor to them. J. C. Broders accepted a call to Brazil and not only served a congregation there but also worked with German pastors already there. The mission effort expanded from Brazil to Argentina. The South America mission field became the Brazil District of the Missouri Synod. By 1922 the District had 50 pastors serving 130 congregations and preaching stations.

Another factor that lowered the German profile in the Missouri Synod was the expansion of the mission work among black people. Through officially this work was done through the Synodical Conference, it eventually became identified with the Missouri Synod.

A favorite story among Black Lutherans in the South tells of three black children playing together.

"I'm an American Baptist," says one.

"I'm a Southern Presbyterian," says the second.

"I'm a German Lutheran," says the third.

Pastor Bakke continued his work in New Orleans, Louisiana, and spread out into southern Mississippi and Alabama. Progress was slow, but congregations were being established.

But the real story of the Lutheran Church in the South is the story of a black woman, Rosa Young of Rosebud, Alabama. Dr. Young (she was awarded a doctor of letters degree from Concordia Seminary, Springfield, in 1963) was born in 1890. There were no public schools for black children in her part of Alabama, though black people paid taxes to support public schools. As a child Dr. Young had a strong interest in education. Through her own efforts she learned to read.

But Dr. Young was not content to get an education only for herself. She wanted to be a teacher and enrolled in Payne University in Selma. That school would be equal to a high school today, but it was higher education then. She had to start to school weeks after others because she had to finish picking the cotton crop before she could leave the farm. In the spring she had to drop out early to help plant cotton. But she made it through school—only to have no job as a teacher back in Rosebud, where she wanted to teach. She made several attempts to begin a school but couldn't get enough money. The black people had no money. Most of the white people were afraid the blacks would "rise above their raisin's," if they learned to read.

Finally, with the help of several white landowners she started a school. There is a story that her school, like Jesus, began its life in a stable. Actually the building was not completed on time (building programs are the same in all times and all places), and she held her first classes in a nearby barn.

There was no money to keep the school in operation. Black parents were willing for their children to attend but could not pay any tuition beyond some food for the teacher. Dr. Young appealed to Booker T. Washington of Tuskegee Institute (100 miles to the east) for help. Dr. Washington could not help, but he suggested that she write to the Lutheran Church in St. Louis. He had heard of the Missouri Synod's interest in elementary education. Synodical officials asked Pastor Bakke to find Rosa Young—and the mission work among black people had a whole new beginning.

Pastor Bakke and Rosa Young became missionary partners. On Palm Sunday and Easter, 1916, 58 people were baptized and 70 were confirmed to be the first Lutheran congregation in Rosebud. The new congregation began with 117 baptized members. In less than a year it had grown to 187, including Rosa Young.

Dr. Young became the key figure in one of the most amazing mission stories of the Missouri Synod. Working against the odds of poverty, racism, and primitive transportation methods, she set out to establish schools for black children. As soon as one school was begun,

DR. ROSA YOUNG   REV. NILS J. BAKKE

she moved on to another. The missionaries of the Synodical Conference were overworked just trying to keep up with her.

The area in which Dr. Young worked is called the Black Belt of
Alabama. The name comes from the strip of black soil that stretches
through the normal Alabama red clay—though many mistakenly assume the name reflects the fact that the majority of the people in that
area are black. Most of the black people were either sharecroppers or
day workers, which means they were paid only for the days they
worked during planting and harvest time. The black people lived on
farms or in small communities with no means of transportation.
Dr. Young and her mission helpers went from village to village, beginning a school and a congregation (in that order) in places with
interesting names like King's Landing and Possum Trot.

The synod recognized the need for a school in the South to train
black pastors and teachers for church work. Early attempts to send
black students to the different climate and culture of the available
synodical schools did not work out. Immanuel Lutheran College was
opened at Concord, North Carolina, in 1903 and moved to Greensboro in 1905. It became the seminary for black students until it was
closed in 1961. Also Luther College, for black students, was opened in

New Orleans in 1903. It closed in 1925. A school that was to become the Alabama Lutheran Academy and College opened in Selma, Alabama, in 1922. Dr. Young was at first a housemother and then was placed on the faculty of the Selma school. It is a part of the Missouri Synod's network of colleges today.

Dr. Young became a popular figure throughout the synod. She traveled and spoke to large groups about her mission work. She wrote the story of her life, *Light in the Black Belt,* which was widely read throughout the synod. Dr. Young's book is embarrassing today for those who want to read the events of 1920 through their 1972 glasses. She tells how white people were her friends, though she always calls them Miss or Mr., but calls black friends by their first names. She calmly accepts racial prejudice even in the church with no bitterness. But she spoke for her time. The education she provided for the children in those times made it possible for many of the advances in racial relations that have occurred since.

Let's conclude the story of Dr. Young beyond the span of the history we are now covering. When cotton was dethroned in the South and industry expanded in the North, most of the black people left the areas of the South where Dr. Young had worked. That part of Alabama now has many ghost villages, where the cotton farms have been converted to tree farms. Among the old remaining, unused shacks, are

Lutheran Church in Alabama grew out of the Synod's earlier efforts to reach out to Americans of non-German heritage – southern blacks.

(Mission Education Photo)

many Lutheran churches. But some remain yet today. Congregations have merged. There are several large new Lutheran churches and schools in rural Alabama to give present-day evidence of Dr. Young's work. Also many congregations in northern cities have been formed by Lutherans who moved from Alabama.

Honors were given to Dr. Young. When the Missouri Synod assumed ownership of the Alabama Lutheran Academy and College in Selma, a new girls dorm was built and named Rosa Young Hall. The building includes an apartment planned for Dr. Young to use for the rest of her life. However, after the dedication ceremonies she asked someone to take her back to her sister's home near Rosebud. School authorities explained that she was to live in the apartment.

"There's no place to raise turnips here," she said and went home.

I am going to be personal now, because there is no other way to tell the following story. One of the privileges of my life has been to know Rosa Young. While preparing a Mission:Life course that included a lesson about her, I became one of the last people from the church beyond her own congregation to visit her.

A rickety bridge and narrow dirt road led to her home—this was in 1970. The house, as many homes of rural black people in Alabama, was poor but clean. No paint, built up on rock pillars with chickens beneath, and a turnip patch out back. The walls were covered with newsclippings (not about Dr. Young but about her students), awards, and the usual mementos that those who teach children collect. A missionary to the last, she greeted a fellow pastor and me by asking,

"Why aren't you preachers out working?"

She told of her experiences over the years in a voice that was too low for the tape recorder. She had spent only one night in jail—that was because she had been in the home of white Christians. But her short jail record and lack of shipwrecks seemed to be the only areas where her sufferings were less than those of the apostle Paul. When we were ready to leave I asked her,

"Dr. Young, of all the things that have happened to you, what has been the most important?"

"Teaching the children about Jesus," she answered. "Tell them that's what counts."

All of the saints in the Missouri Synod have clearly shown their humanity in its various manifestations. But nowhere has the humanness come through with such beauty as in Dr. Rosa Young of Rosebud, Alabama. She died June 30, 1971.

By 1922 there were 49 organized congregations and 8 preaching stations in the Negro mission field. There were 95 workers—only 23 of them white. The Selma school had six students, all girls.

As though the term black Lutherans wasn't enough to prove that the Missouri Synod had outworn its German title, let's look at another reason for the name change.

In 1911 the Missouri Synod held its convention in St. Louis at Holy Cross Lutheran Church, near the seminary, publishing house, and hospital. At the same time the English Synod held its convention at Redeemer Lutheran Church, a few blocks away. All Districts of the Missouri Synod were using the English language, with 400 pastors preaching the official language of America. Obviously the time had come for the Missouri and English Synods to merge.

But how? The English Synod wasn't anxious to be swallowed up by Missouri. The solution was that the English Synod became a non-geographical district of the Missouri Synod, meaning that it was to function as a district across the geographical boundaries of the other districts. Careful arrangements were worked out to prevent the congregations from competing with one another. The English Synod's schools, in Conover, North Carolina, and Winfield, Kansas, were given to the Missouri Synod. Numerous synodical conventions since have made committees consider the "Amalgamation of the English District," but the synod has continued to see a need for the special work of a nongeographic district.

At the time of the merger the English Synod publication *The Lutheran Witness* became the official English publication of the Missouri Synod. The adopted child soon outgrew the natural-born child, *Der Lutheraner.*

Already in 1905 Concordia Publishing House had published the "gray hymnal" in English, but it was a concession for "minority groups." However, the gray hymnal paved the way for the *Evangelical Lutheran Hymnbook* of 1912, previously published by the English Synod. It was printed in two editions, one with music and one without. The "without" edition was the "black hymnal" used for years by many congregations and still available in some parishes.

The English District also invited the Missouri Synod to Sunday school. Though a few Missouri congregations had started Sunday schools, they were mostly just *Christenlehre* at a different hour. The chief Missouri Synod objections to Sunday school were: (1) Sunday schools used lay teachers. Missouri felt that all church teachers had to have theological training. (2) There was no orthodox material available. They would not use lessons prepared by other denominations. However, the English District had its own material, "Little Lambs," that was also given to the synod. (3) Sunday schools might be used as an excuse for parents not to send their children to the Christian day schools. All of these arguments gradually broke down. By 1920 there were 1,587 Sunday schools in the synod. There were over 3,000 in 1932.

If you looked at the map of districts at the beginning of the chapter (p. 73) you noted that more districts had been established. Also notice that most of the expansion was in the Midwest. The synod had decided that "home" (the official name that had replaced "inner") missions would be carried on by the districts. It was felt that mission committees on a district level would have a better understanding about the location of new mission congregations. Also established congregations would be more apt to support new mission congregations if they were nearer home. The district control of mission expansion did help spread the synod's work evenly throughout the Midwest. However, it did not help much in the outlying areas of the synod. Areas that had fewer congregations had less mission money and therefore established fewer new stations.

A program which began in 1902 became the financial strength for future mission development — the Church Extension Fund. This fund was established to loan money at low interest to new congregations for land and buildings. The trouble was that 4 years later the fund had a balance of only $400. Offerings from the celebration of the 100th anniversary of Walther's birth in 1911 gave the fund a big boost to $44,400. By 1919 the Church Extension Fund had helped finance 260 buildings. But its income was by donation only.

Now for education: Naturally, the synod moved a few schools around. In 1909 the school in the East dedicated its new buildings in the new location of Bronxville, New York, where it is at present. The teachers college in Addison was moved to nearby River Forest, Illinois, in 1913. Two new Concordias were opened by districts on the West Coast: in Portland, Oregon, in 1905, and in Oakland, California, in 1906. The first Concordia in Canada opened in 1921 in Edmonton, Alberta. In 1919 the teachers college in Seward accepted its first female students.

Social ministries continued to operate on the fringe of the synodical structure. There were several unsuccessful attempts to bring the areas of special ministry under the synod's administration. Instead the Associated Lutheran Charities arose in 1904. The association helped provide a unity among the social ministries and provided material and training for church workers in special areas.

Another first occurred in 1899 when the Western District called F. W. Herzberger as the first full-time city missionary. His mission was not to establish a congregation but to minister to people in hospitals, jails, and other public institutions.

Herzberger and Philip Wambsganss (the son of one of the first four Lutheran deaconesses in the United States) introduced the deaconess program to the Missouri Synod. Working through the Associated Lutheran Charities they established the Lutheran Deaconess Association in 1919. A deaconess house was bought and located at the Lutheran Hospital in Fort Wayne, Ind. At that time all deaconesses were nurses. In a short time other deaconess training centers were founded in Wisconsin and Kansas; however, they later merged with the one in Fort Wayne.

World War I also provided an opportunity for Missouri Synod pastors to become involved in a new ministry—as military chaplains. Though many in the synod objected to ministers serving in a government capacity, three of synod's clergy wore the uniform and served in the military.

The Walther League also became involved in social ministry. In 1904 the league provided a tent for the tuberculosis tent colony at Wheat Ridge, Colorado, near Denver. This project eventually developed into a hospital for tuberculosis patients and was supported by the Walther League through the annual distribution of Christmas seals.

The Walther League also accepted girls into membership during this quarter and began involving younger youth. In 1920 the synod officially recognized the league as a part of the synodical program and appointed a Board for Young People's Work. Walther League headquarters were established in Milwaukee in 1913 and moved to Chicago in 1922.

Another league that was to become an important agency of the synod arose in 1917. During the synodical convention that year a group of laymen were together in the home of Fred Pritzlaff in Milwaukee. They discussed the problem of a $100,000 deficit in the synod's treasury. They organized the Lutheran Laymen's League, which they thought would be temporary, to pay off the deficit. After the $100,000 was raised they established a project of collecting $3 million as a thankoffering at the end of World War I. Though they received only slightly more than $2 million, the fund was a great boost for synod's program. Laymen realized the need for a continued organization, and the Lutheran Laymen's League stayed on the synodical scene.

Concordia Publishing House printed Schwan's (prepared by the former president of the synod) Catechism in 1899. With Luther's Small Catechism in the front and a longer question and answer section as a teaching guide for the six chief parts, this book became the standard text for Lutherans in confirmation classes.

In 1907 Edmund Seuel became the general manager of Concordia Publishing House. He also served as the synodical treasurer for years. Because of his dual capacity the synod's business offices were in the publishing house's building; the synodical president continued to have an office in Chicago.

In 1910 the first *Lutheran Annual* appeared. *The . . . Annual,* which has truly been an annual publication ever since, listed all pastors, teachers, and other church workers in the synod, along with congregations.

The Missouri Synod watched other Lutheran bodies merge during its third quarter. In 1918 the United Lutheran Church was formed: a collection of many of the synods in the old General Synod, the General Council, and the Lutheran Church of the South that was begun during the Civil War. After reaching a high of about 260 different Lutheran synods in the United States, the number now started to edge down as mergers occurred. A group in the Wisconsin Synod attempted to unite the synods in the Synodical Conference in 1914. However, the convention of the entire Wisconsin Synod would not approve the suggestion, so it never came before the Synodical Conference.

As we have finished looking over the years from 1897 to 1922, we might mention just a few customs you probably would have shared had you belonged to the Missouri Synod during that time.

Your pastor would probably have worn a *beffchen* with a black robe, when he conducted the worship services. The *beffchen* was a European custom. It fastened around the pastor's neck and had two white ribbons that extended down from his throat in an upside down V. The black robe would not have been close fitting at the waist as cassocks are today but would not have been as full as the preaching robes of a generation later. The Prince Albert coat worn by Walther and other early clergy had almost disappeared from the scene.

Your congregation would probably have had Communion only once a quarter; though some congregations had monthly celebrations of the Sacrament since the founding of the synod. In many churches you would have received the bread on one side of the altar, then gone behind the altar to the other side to receive the wine. There may have been an offering plate behind the altar for you to contribute for the purchase of bread and wine. This started as a symbol of an earlier custom when church members provided the bread and wine from their homes. But it soon degenerated into another offering.

Your children may have had a Sunday school, but it is doubtful that there would have been classes for adults. Men sat on one side of the church during the worship service while the women sat on the other. Like many other customs this was not a rule, but it took a brave person to break the custom.

But insurance would have been a matter of conscience for you. Though the Missouri Synod never made it official, many within the synod condemned all forms of insurance because it failed to show trust in God. For years no synodical property was insured. Others approved of insurance on property, because a cash value could be established, but were against life insurance. As life insurance policies became more of an investment than a gamble, the opposition to insurance declined.

VIII. Putting It All Together
(Or "I Suppose You Wonder Why I Called This Meeting")

Our tour has arrived at 1947. It was the year before Harry S Truman surprised everyone but himself by defeating Thomas Dewey for the presidency of the United States. The whole world was readjusting to a hopeful but yet uncomfortable peace that followed World War II, the "war to end all wars, number two." The split between East and West was developing. With the memory of two atomic explosions that ended World War II fresh in their minds, the people of 1947 wanted a lasting peace. The United Nations became a symbol of hope while the Truman Doctrine of 1947, promising United States aid to nations resisting communism, was a sign of reality. At the same time the Marshall Plan to help rebuild war-torn countries showed the continued price of war.

And the Missouri Synod celebrated its 100th anniversary.

First let's catch up on the statistics for the last 25 years. In the 1920s the synod increased 15%, 24% in the 30s, and 29% in the 40s. In 1947 there were 1,567,453 baptized members in 4,429 congregations in 33 districts. The Missouri Synod had congregations in all 48 states (the last state was Arizona where a congregation began in 1939) and in two territories: congregations in Alaska in 1926 and in Hawaii in 1945.

President Pfotenhauer was 76 years old at the 1935 convention in Cleveland, Ohio. His family and friends encouraged him to follow the example of previous presidents and decline renomination for the office he had held for 24 years. However, Pfotenhauer felt that if he refused to run he would be influencing the synod's decision on his successor. To him it was a matter for the convention to decide. The elections were held by eliminating candidates with the least number of votes and continuing to ballot until one candidate received more than 50% of the votes cast. After four ballots, John W. Behnken was elected to replace Dr. Pfotenhauer.

Behnken was the first American-born president of the Missouri

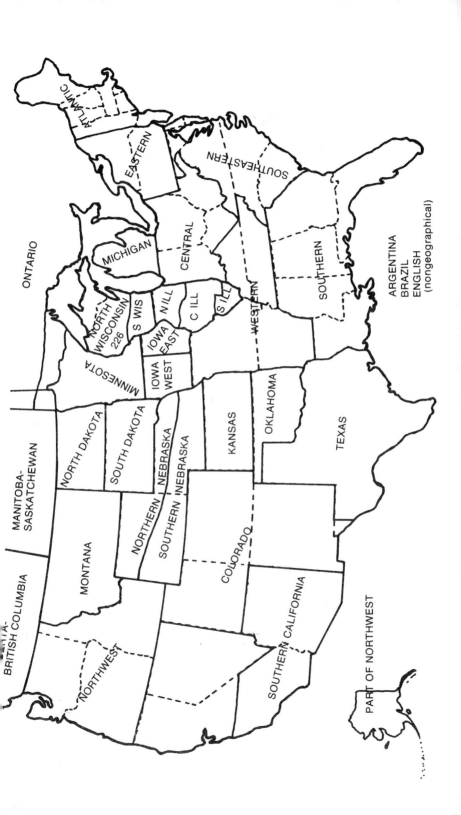

DR. JOHN W. BEHNKEN

Synod. He was a Texan in all ways: born there, served congregations there, and he had been president of the Texas District before becoming vice-president of the Synod in 1929.

The years from 1922 to 1947 challenged the Missouri Synod to put its practice where its theology was. During its birth pains and adolescent struggles Missouri had placed a lot of meaning on the word synod. Coming from the Greek, synod means those who walk together; not only are they united in existence, but they are also united in action. The unity of the Missouri Synod has always been a prized, but mysterious, part of that segment of Lutheranism. The unity has not prevented infighting with all the heated debates, printed attacks, and name-calling that goes with disunity. It seems that the brothers, and in recent years sisters, in the Missouri Synod use those family relationships not as images of people piously singing hymns together, but as the human family situation of brothers and sisters who do scrap but also truly love one another.

Anyway, unity has been a part of the Missouri Synod. Members of the synod generally take it for granted and often show little outward concern about keeping it. Those who watch the Missouri Synod from the outside alternate between marveling at the unity and predicting that the unity will soon come to an end.

That unity of the Missouri Synod had to be examined and defined during the fourth quarter of its history. In the early years the unity was more simple because many bonds contributed to its strength. The synod had been a small group, they all knew one another either personally or by name through others. The intermarriage of families in the synod would make an interesting book in itself. They had spoken the same language in a world that spoke a different language. Though there were two seminaries they were near each other both geographically and theologically. Any rivalry between the two (and there was and is much rivalry) was that of two brothers vying for attention from Mom. Since all of the synod's clergy graduated from the two seminaries, there was a predictable uniformity among synod's pastors.

As the synod grew all of this closeness began to change. It was not just that Germans learned to speak English. But there were people who had never spoken German. People of other national backgrounds were becoming an active part of the synod. And that new breed, Americans who identified with no "old country" were becoming numerous in the church.

Harry Smith, a retired salesman and full-time lay worker for a Lutheran Church in Florida, has told how he was the first English speaking student in the Lutheran college in Milwaukee back in the early 1930s. His professors and classmates had trouble with his name and often called him Schmitt. When he corrected them, they would ask why he had changed it. They did not know that as a teen-ager he had attended a funeral of a friend in a Lutheran church. He was so impressed by the joy of the Gospel message that he became a Lutheran.

Perhaps the story of Harry Smith and his classmates is typical of the Missouri Synod during the 1930s and into the 40s. Like an adolescent who is unaware of his recent growth and is surprised that furniture breaks when he jumps on it, the synod members were surprised that fellow Americans responded favorably to their church. Their theology had survived intact its translation not only into the English language but also into the American culture. After years of fearing the leap into a new world and a new century they were happy to find the environment not so cold after all.

But this awareness of a new acceptance also brought new responsibilities. The word synod can have another emphasis. In some denominations, as well as in Lutheran history, a synod is a meeting. Missouri had satisfied itself that it had sufficient reasons for being a synod, or for "calling a meeting." But now it had to explain to others why it had called the meeting named Missouri.

In the first place, it had to define its relationship with other Lutheran bodies. In 1918 eight Lutheran synods, including over half of all American Lutherans, had formed the National Lutheran Council, a cooperative group that did not imply pulpit (we preach at your church and you preach at ours) or altar (we commune at your church and you commune at ours) fellowship. Missouri Synod did not join the national council.

Yet there was a bond between the Lutherans of the Missouri Synod and others, especially those in the Ohio, Iowa, and Buffalo Synods as well as other small groups not officially included in the Synodical Conference. Before these synods organized, the groups involved had recognized one another as people on the same mission. Both groups grew in the same parts of the country. Missouri (more stable according to one point of view, more stubborn according to another) stayed in its own organization, made its own plans, and did its own thing. The other groups did more changing around as they tried to build a nest for all American Lutherans. They went through frequent organizational realignments and federations (less concerned about true doctrine according to one view, more willing to try something new according to another).

The old problem of accepting all of the Lutheran Confessions and nothing but the Lutheran Confessions had largely been solved. Most of the Lutheran groups in the United States had given up on the efforts to unite Reformed and Lutheran bodies. Those who had continued to combine Lutheran and Reformed doctrine and traditions gradually lost their Lutheran identification. The friction among Lutheran groups was not so much in doctrine, at least not in doctrinal statements, but in practice.

Naturally practice varied from congregation to congregation within the synods. But in general those in the Missouri Synod felt the others were lax on the lodge issue and on Communion practices. Since these two issues became the measuring stick by which Missouri measured the quality of Lutheranism in others, it will be worthwhile for us to look at them briefly.

Discussions and articles about lodge membership often got distracted to issues of weird oaths, the right to belong to a secret society, and unusual morality (the promise not to commit adultery with another lodge member's wife). But the true issue centered on the teaching that Christ is the only way of salvation. Many lodges, especially Masons, teach a way of salvation without Christ. At one time most denominations taught that there was a contradiction between such a lodge and

Christianity. All Lutheran bodies have objected to lodge membership as a denial of the Gospel. But objection has been registered in different ways. Most Missouri Synod congregations (and some others) have required lodge members to drop their membership before joining the church. Other Lutheran groups (and some Missouri Synod congregations) teach that the church should confront people with the contradiction but that lodge membership in itself should not prevent membership in the church. Walther did not approve of lodge membership but saw it as a pastoral matter rather than a constitutional issue. Other Lutherans often felt that the Missouri Synod was legalistic on the matter of lodges. The Missouri Synod accused other Lutherans of agreeing with a position but not practicing it.

Communion practice presented a similar problem. All agreed on the doctrines involved. In receiving the bread and wine one also receives the body and blood of Christ — not because the receiver believes it to be so but because Christ the giver has made it so. Also all Lutherans agreed that those who do not know the meaning of the Sacrament should not receive it. Some Missouri Synod congregations practiced close Communion that required announcements prior to communing. This seemed legalistic to others. Other Lutherans had various practices but were primarily concerned with announcing what the Sacrament was at each service so people would know what they were receiving. This did not seem like enough instruction for Missourians.

These two issues have been oversimplified. There were also other issues. Some Missourians talked about prayer fellowship — they would not pray with anyone with whom they were not in complete doctrinal agreement. Others in the same synod objected to such divisions. Though the Missouri Synod was accused of being legalistic on doctrinal matters, Missourians often thought the other synods were pietistic on such issues as use of alcoholic beverages, playing cards, working on Sunday, dancing, etc. However, for a while some Missouri Synod clergy also strongly opposed dancing of any kind.

But these differences were small compared to the great body of doctrine and practice that Lutherans held in common. Years earlier Lutherans had found a way to talk together without ruffling fellowship feathers. They would call a free conference by announcing that a given subject or doctrine would be discussed. Members of various synods would go to hear what the other guy had to say and to give his own theological views — all unofficial. When agreements were reached at free conferences, they could then brave the chance of official representation.

Between 1918 and 1920 there were six official meetings of representatives of Ohio, Iowa, Wisconsin, and Missouri Synods. They worked through a number of problems and finally adopted the *Chicago Theses* in 1925. These theses dealt with the subjects that had caused disagreement among the synods and were to be presented to each synod's convention.

The Missouri Synod appointed a committee to study the *Chicago Theses* at their 1926 convention. The report of the committee at the 1929 convention rejected the theses. Wisconsin Synod did the same. In 1930 the other synods, Iowa, Ohio, and Buffalo united as the American Lutheran Church, which is not the same as the present ALC which is *The* American Lutheran Church.

In 1932 the Missouri Synod convention adopted *A Brief Statement*, a brief Scriptural statement of the doctrinal position of the Missouri Synod. This statement was largely the work of Dr. Francis Pieper, the former president of synod. The *Brief Statement* was never accepted as an addition to the Lutheran Confessions yet it was given a position similar to them. Other Lutherans regarded this as widening the split between Missouri and themselves.

But the Missouri Synod did not forget its long, if troubled relationship with the Lutherans in the ALC. By 1935 the Missouri Synod and the ALC were again having meetings. The ALC had no disagreements with *A Brief Statement* but did not want to adopt it as an addition to the Lutheran Confessions. Meanwhile the ALC also had its statement, the *Minneapolis Theses,* as the basis for the groups that merged in 1932.

To add to the picture, the United Lutheran Church had adopted the *Savannah Declaration* that said there should be no more statements to define Lutheran doctrine but a return to the Confessions that came from the time of the Reformation. At the 1938 convention of the Missouri Synod discussions regarding fellowship with the United Lutheran Church were approved.

Then pressure on Missouri came from a new direction. The Wisconsin Synod and the Norwegian Synod objected to Missouri having discussions with the ALC and the ULC. In 1946 the ALC accepted a policy of "selective fellowship" (congregations of different synods would establish fellowship on a local basis if their practices were in agreement). And the United Lutheran Church said there was no reason for further fellowship discussions since they would have fellowship with anyone who would accept the Lutheran Confessions.

In 1947 the Missouri Synod rejected fellowship with the ALC.

In all of this maneuvering among the Lutheran groups it is obvious that each group had mixed feelings about the issues that separated them and the issues that united them. It is easy to think of each group as a corporate being having trouble making up its mind. In reality, of course, each group was made up of many individuals whose minds were made up. The struggle for a corporate decision indicates a struggle of the many members of each group.

We have spoken of a unity in the Missouri Synod. As the synod struggled in its relationship with the Synodical Conference and with other Lutheran groups it is obvious there was also disunity — or at least there was more than one view on subjects.

The existence of at least two views was clearly shown in 1945 when 44 pastors signed *A Statement,* soon known as the "Statement of the 44." In 12 theses the statement affirmed historic Lutheran positions on Scripture, the use of the Gospel, the Holy Christian church as a body of all believers in Christ, place of the local congregation, and the like. But *A Statement* also deplored a legalistic use of doctrines, misuse of certain Bible verses regarding unionism, the attitude that the Missouri Synod was the only true church on earth, and certain methods of deciding fellowship issues.

It was the year of the atomic bomb, and the "Statement of the 44" was Missouri's own atomic bomb. Many welcomed the *Statement* as evidence of a side of Missouri that they said had always existed. They quoted Walther and the church fathers on their side. Others deplored the *Statement* as a new teaching. They quoted Walther and Pieper on their side. One pastor claimed that each of the 12 theses contained false doctrines. The 44 signers, including five seminary professors, four district presidents, and a retired seminary president, were heroes to some and villains to others. Pastoral conferences and district conventions debated the issues.

Theological issues raised in the *Statement* were regarded as a threat to the unity of the synod. Some feared an open split. The synodical president, Dr. Behnken, persuaded the 44 to withdraw the *Statement* on the basis of procedural not doctrinal error. The writers did not deny the *Statement;* they said that their method of presenting their concerns may not have been proper. This solution eased the tension.

Few Missourians would find false teachings in the *Statement* today, though some might. The *Statement* was never reintroduced, but many of the 44 signers have since attained positions of high leadership in the synod. Their view was obviously representative of many in the synod.

The "Statement of the 44" showed there were two views in the synod. But it is difficult to simply state those two views in a way that both sides accept as a definition of the problem. Maybe the problem was and is that those involved have never agreed on the problem. Each side wants to define not only their position but also the other's. One side sees itself as theologically correct according to the Lutheran Confessions and sees the others as liberals who deny or ignore Biblical truths. The other side sees itself as evangelical and pastoral but views the opposition as rigid and legalistic.

The question is: When someone asks, "Will the real Missouri Synod please stand?" does one theology stand or two? Are there two positions, or are they two sides of the same coin? The answers are not in the back of the book.

But Missouri's reason for "calling a meeting" was not just to argue theology. The redeeming feature of the synod, that kept it alive and excited during the times of theological struggle, is that it also faced its relationship to the world in which it existed. During its fourth quarter the synod became much more involved in a mission and ministry to the world.

In its early years the synod had depended upon immigrants from Europe for its membership growth. The influx of European Lutherans was so great that the Missouri Synod was able to reach only a small percentage of the immigrants. However the flow of newcomers dwindled to a trickle in the early 1900s, and Missouri's rate of growth dropped to its lowest point from 1910 to 1930.

But there was some growth — an indication that people other than German Lutherans would join the synod. Through marriage, and through the work of individual pastors and lay people adults without church membership or from other denominations were coming into the Missouri Synod. About 3,000 adults joined the synod each year in the first quarter of this century. There were no organized evangelism efforts. When the word evangelist was used in synodical publications it was always in the negative sense — to warn members about the dangers of the emotional approach of evangelists. All evangelism was seen as part of the sawdust trail of revivalism.

In the early 30s the synod conducted its first program of what would be called evangelism today, though the word was not used. Materials for the effort, "Call of the Hour," were printed in both German and English. By present-day standards it wasn't much of an effort. There was little promotion or organization. But it was a beginning. In 1931 over 700 adults became new members of the synod.

The synod also increased its ministry to the American public by going into radio broadcasting. In 1923 the Board of Control of the St. Louis seminary started plans to build a Lutheran radio station. With help from the Lutheran Laymen's League, the Walther League, and other Lutheran groups in the St. Louis area the funds were raised and KFUO opened with its first broadcast on September 26, 1924.

In October 1930 The Lutheran Hour started as a regular Thursday evening broadcast on 38 stations from coast to coast — again with funds from the Lutheran Laymen's League. Though there was a greater-than-expected response, the program had to be dropped in June of 1931 because of lack of funds — younger readers should be reminded that there was a financial depression then. But the idea wasn't forgotten. Early in 1935 The Lutheran Hour was back on the air from Detroit and Cincinnati stations. By 1939 the program was on 99 stations. When the broadcasting industry developed a way to record programs for later broadcast the number of stations carrying the program jumped to 682 by 1944. The Lutheran Hour went international in 1944-45 and was broadcast in three languages in 25 countries.

Antenna Wires of radio station KFUO stretch over Concordia Seminary, 1924.

DR. W. A. MAIER

Dr. Walter A. Maier, a professor at the St. Louis seminary, was The Lutheran Hour speaker from its beginning. He became a nationally known figure—the first Missouri Synod Lutheran to reach such prominence. His rapid delivery and frequent quotations from the Bible gave his broadcast a distinctive quality. His messages were always evangelistic in that they confronted each hearer with the news of Christ's victory over sin and death and asked for a response.

The number of adults joining the church each year increased—over 10,000 for the first time in 1938. The Lutheran Hour not only brought people to the church, but it also showed pastors and lay people that their message was in demand.

During the 1930s about one million dollars a year came into the synodical treasury. Though the great depression of the early 30s limited local and district work it did not seriously lower the synodical income. During the low income years an editorial in *The Lutheran Witness* commented on the shortage of money. Lest people think the lack of funds was caused by the depression, the editorial reminded the readers that there had also been shortages in the good financial years before the crash of 1929.

However the financial depression did have a lasting effect on the synod. It pointed out the need for better planning and unified spending. At the 1932 convention the only request for special funds came from the Fort Wayne college. They wanted to put in a short sidewalk. The request was denied because of lack of funds. The growth of the synodical structure in the 40s and 50s can be traced to problems that leaders of the church felt during the depression years, when they saw great needs and could do little or nothing about them.

Synodical officials found themselves in an embarrassing spot in 1939 — a $600,000 deficit. Synod's leaders were conservative not only in theology but also in finances. They didn't like to operate in the red.

The financial need came at a time when there was also a need to celebrate. It had been 100 years since the Saxons arrived in Perry County. The needs were combined in a program "Call of the Cross" which emphasized both evangelism and stewardship. The deficit was wiped out in one year, and the annual offerings to synod increased to about $2 million.

As part of the Saxon centenial observance the synod made its first movie, also called "Call of the Cross." The film was made in St. Louis with local people playing the roles of the early Saxons. The movie was shown over 3,000 times in the first celebration and has been reissued for the 125th anniversary.

The story of synod's schools during this quarter contributed to mission expansion in a rather strange way. Only one new school was opened, another Concordia College, this one in Austin, Texas, in 1926. The St. Louis seminary again outgrew its buildings. The school was moved again, this time to the west side of St. Louis in Clayton, Mo. The new structures were dedicated in 1926 on the site where the seminary is still located. In 1939 both of the teachers colleges (Seward and River Forest) became 4-year schools.

But the real school story was a problem that hit for the first time in 1930 — there were more graduates from the seminaries than were needed by the congregations. The situation continued year after year. The excess of available pastors created a problem for those in the seminary and prep schools. Their training in languages and theology did not prepare them for other occupations. Many of the men had been studying for the ministry since they were in the ninth grade. Some of the unused graduates made the break and entered other occupations — and still provided some of the best trained leadership a congregation has ever had. Others went out and started their own congregations as the only method available for them to become pastors. The amazing fact that many new Missouri Synod congregations were begun during the depression years of the 30s is not due to a mission program but to an oversupply of ministers. It is estimated that 300 congregations made their start in that way.

But the synod wanted to protect its seminary graduates from the possibility of completing their training and not receiving a call. At the 1935 convention the delegates voted 266 to 265 to close the Springfield seminary. But the close vote troubled many, so it was brought to the convention again. The seminary remained open by a second vote — 283 to 256. There were several other attempts to close the Springfield seminary and several pretheological schools. However only the school in Conover, North Carolina, was closed during that time.

In 1939 the synod appointed an Armed Services Commission to supervise the work of chaplains. When the Second World War began, the Missouri Synod was ready to provide chaplains. The increased need for pastors because of the number entering the chaplaincy helped decrease the backlog of available clergy. During the war 253 Missouri Synod pastors were chaplains in the United States military forces and five in the Canadian military. By the war's end the supply and demand ratio of available clergy was again in balance. A few years later there was a shortage of ministers.

Military chaplains also increased Missouri Synod's profile in the American way of life. Through chaplains many people, especially those from non-Lutheran parts of the country had their first contact with the Lutheran Church. The Missouri Synod was the only major denomination that attempted to keep in regular contact by mail with all of its members in the military service. Each person entering a branch of the armed forces received a Lutheran "dog tag," a prayer book, and other reading material. In addition, their addresses were given to the chaplains serving their bases and to pastors in the area. Many new Missouri Synod congregations were founded near military bases.

In a similar way the Missouri Synod became more involved on college campuses during the second quarter of this century. In 1926 the synod decided to appoint a field secretary for the Student Welfare Committee; but it was 1940 before the first secretary, Reuben Hahn, filled the office. Like military chaplains, campus pastors became a source of contact for the synod with many people.

Shortages of manpower and material delayed mission expansion during the war. However, synodical leaders made plans for a Peace Thankoffering as soon as the war ended. When peace in Europe was declared, President Behnken visited the areas that had been bombed and where battles had been fought. He reestablished contact with the churches of Europe in fellowship with the Missouri Synod. He found many of the people in Europe in great need and immediately requested members of the synod in the United States to help. Faced with two special offerings in the same year members of the synod responded far beyond expected goals. The Peace Thankoffering received over $6 million; this went for mission expansion. Another $1.3 million was given to the relief offering for fellow Lutherans in Europe.

The Lutheran Laymen's League grew rapidly during the 30s and 40s. Starting as a synodwide organization, the league formed local congregational clubs in 1929. The first was at Grace Lutheran Church, Fargo, North Dakota. The 1,000th club joined the league in 1947. It was an agency of First Lutheran Church, Little Rock, Arkansas.

The Walther League's major effort continued to be the support of Wheat Ridge hospital. The youth also began the *Walther League Messenger* and produced the first *Walther League Manual*.

At the beginning of the fourth quarter the women in the Missouri Synod had no synodical organization, though most local congregations had a ladies aid. In 1928 women from six congregations met in Oklahoma City to organize the Lutheran Women's League of Oklahoma. They began the use of mite boxes that later became a national project. In 1930 the synod approved the formation of a National Women's League, but repeated delays caused the matter to be dropped. In 1942 the national organization of what was to become the Lutheran Women's Missionary League appeared on the synodical scene.

These three agencies: for men, women, and youth, contributed not only to the spiritual growth and Christian service of the synod but also to its social life. Going to a "league" meeting became a part of the congregational activities of many church members. Going to a league convention often became a way for lay people to become involved in district and synodical activities and to become acquainted with fellow members of synod in other congregations.

In 1925 the Missouri Synod entered a new field of education, when a group of laymen purchased Valparaiso University in Valparaiso, Indiana. The school had been begun in the mid-1800s by the Methodist Church. In turn it had become a private school that used many experimental educational methods; then it was almost sold to the Klu Klux Klan. But representatives of the Missouri Synod bought it as the first, and still the only, Missouri Synod university. Though not synodical property, it was placed under a board of directors who were members of the synod. Valparaiso University has remained closely affiliated with the synod and has educated many professional and lay church workers.

The overseas mission program expanded from 1922 to 1947. Though the war caused mission work in China to decrease, missionaries were sent to eight additional countries.

Perhaps the most exciting new mission field was Nigeria. In 1928 Christians in that African country sent Jonathan Udo Ekong to the United States to receive a theological education. After examining a number of schools Ekong selected Immanuel Lutheran College at Greensboro, South Carolina. While in the school, Ekong became interested in the Lutheran Church and asked the Synodical Conference to send missionaries to his country. A committee, including Henry Nau who had been a missionary to India for the synod, was sent to Nigeria to investigate the request. Not only did the committee suggest that mission work be started in Nigeria, but Nau was the first missionary to go. By 1947 the Lutheran Church in Nigeria had over 10,000 baptized members.

Concordia Publishing House also had a part in the increase of evangelism awareness in the synod. In 1937 a series of daily devotions were printed for Lent. The series was widely used, even beyond synodical lines, and was continued under various titles. In 1947 the daily devotional series was named *Portals of Prayer,* with a German edition, *Taegliche Andachten.* The series later had the largest circulation of any Missouri Synod publication: over one million copies per issue in English and another 27,000 in German. O. A. Dorn replaced Edmund Seuel as general manager of the publishing house in 1944.

When the synod was founded in 1847 the synodical secretary was also the church historian—the minutes of the conventions were the chief source of history. As the church grew, the need for more complete records for historical research became obvious. In 1927 Concordia Historical Institute was organized and has developed as the chief archives for the synod.

Through many efforts that would now be called evangelism became a part of the synod during the 30s and 40s, the term evangelism and its related words did not gain acceptance until after World War II. *Today* magazine, a synodical publication dating from 1946, edited by Herman Gockel, helped give evangelism general acceptance. Filled with practical "how to" articles *Today* was directed to the congregation and local mission work. Though it existed for only a few years, and was later replaced by *Advance* magazine, *Today* contributed to the mission awareness of many members of the Missouri Synod.

The synod had changed its name in 1917, but most members still weren't satisfied with, and few used, the long title of Evangelical Lutheran Synod of Missouri, Ohio, and Other States. Even the initials, ELSMOOS, as you can see, didn't improve the image.

Numerous suggestions were made for possible new names. But the obvious solution was to adopt the nickname that had come into common usage "Missouri Synod." Others said that "Missouri" was misleading since there is no special connection between the synod and the state. Yet others argued that 100 years of usage had given Missouri a special meaning not only in the church at large but also in the world. Many did not want the synod to lose that special identification.

At the 1944 convention the name The Lutheran Church, Missouri Synod was selected, but it was turned down by a congregational referendum. In 1947 the name The Lutheran Church—Missouri Synod was approved by the convention and also by a referendum of the congregations.

Had you been a member of a Missouri Synod congregation from 1922 to 1947 you would have seen many changes. There is a new hymnal, *The Lutheran Hymnal*. Though it is available in many colors most church members regard it as the blue hymnal. First printed in 1941 the new hymnal contained the music with the hymns.

By 1947 your pastor was probably wearing a Geneva gown during the worship services. Though it is really an academic vestment, it became a "preaching gown" to Lutherans by usage. It was black with many pleats and full sleeves.

If your congregation was typical it had increased Communion services to at least once a month by 1947. Many Lutherans were taught to kneel at a Communion rail for the Sacrament. Altars were back against the wall. Families were now sitting together on either side of the church—except for grandma and grandpa who probably preferred to remain women on the left, men on the right. Sunday school was the accepted thing—even for adults. Women still did not attend voters meetings or hold church offices.

Missouri was a hundred years old—but it didn't look its age.

IX. Rejoicing in Mercy
(Or "Missouri, You've Come a Long Way")

Our tour has reached its goal, 1972, the 125th anniversary of the founding of The Lutheran Church — Missouri Synod. Recent history is difficult history, because it is news that has not had time to rise properly before being baked into a neat loaf of history. Yet yesterday's news is today's history, so we need to look at what happened since 1947.

It is already history that Richard Nixon was reelected president after defeating George McGovern in the greatest presidential landslide in the history of the United States. By the way, 48 was not the final number of states. There are now 50. In the last 25 years the country has participated in two unusual wars — unusual in that officially they were not wars, but actually they were the most destructive, most expensive, longest lasting wars the nation has ever had — the Korean Conflict of the 50s and the Vietnam Era of the 60s and 70s. The unrest of a nation that has gone through a racial revolution (the end of which is not yet seen) and endured a new confrontation on moral issues of drugs, abortion, pollution, and war, has also spilled over into the church.

The space age promise that we are a part of mankind's giant leap because one man stepped on the moon seems to go unfulfilled as the space program winds down with the attitude, "now that we've done it, it wasn't so much fun after all."

And the Missouri Synod celebrates its 125th anniversary with the theme, "Rejoicing in Mercy." Again a touch of sober reality. Not "Rejoice, 'cause we've made it," not "Rejoice, 'cause God has done great things through us," but "Rejoice in mercy" — an honest look at 125 years of history sees the abiding mercy of Jesus Christ as the only comfort for sins of wrong action and nonaction, and the only explanation for the successes that have been achieved.

And there have been measurable successes. In the 1950s the synod increased by 65%; it had a 24% increase of membership in the 60s. The

synod entered its anniversary year with 2,797,298 baptized members in the United States and 88,909 in Canada. Members in the two South American districts make the total over 3 million. There are 5,760 congregations in the United States and 334 in Canada.

On the map of districts (p. 105) you will see additional changes. Of the four original districts, only the Eastern still exists. Both the Western and the Central Districts were subdivided in the last 25 years. There is another nongeographical district. The Slovak Synod (which had changed its name to the Synod of Evangelical Lutheran Churches, SELC) became the SELC District of the Missouri Synod in 1971, with provisions that it would be assimiliated into the geographical districts within 7 years.

In the fifth quarter of a century of its history (as in its third) the synod had three presidents. Dr. John W. Behnken continued as president until the Cleveland convention in 1962, when he asked not to be renominated. Dr. Oliver Harms was elected to replace him. Dr. Harms followed Behnken's footsteps in many ways. He had been pastor of Trinity, Houston, where Behnken also had been pastor. Harms had been president of the Texas District and vice-president of the synod, offices that Behnken had also held.

At the Denver convention in 1969, Dr. Jacob A. O. Preus (his father had served two terms as governor of Minnesota) was elected president of the Missouri Synod. Of Norwegian descent, Preus had belonged to the Evangelical Lutheran Synod (which was formerly the Norwegian Synod) until 1957, when he became a professor at Concordia Seminary in Springfield. He became the president of the Springfield seminary in 1962.

Let's take a last look at the areas that we have watched develop in the synod.

First the mission field: In the last 25 years the Missouri Synod started various mission activities in 14 additional countries, And — bad news — it discontinued work in one country. Because of the communist takeover of China in 1952 all missionaries had to leave. However, much of this work was continued when mission work was started in Macao and Taiwan. Also the Brazil District initiated a mission project in Portugal. All together the synod has mission efforts in 34 world areas in its anniversary year.

Not only the areas of mission work but also the concept of mission work has expanded. On January 8, 1958, the mission field in India became the Indian Evangelical Lutheran Church — a sister church to the Missouri Synod. In quick succession other overseas missions

Change of Presidents occurs at synodical convention in Denver as Dr. Oliver R. Harms, right, congratulates his successor, Dr. J. A. O. Preus.

became sister churches. The change in status meant that the churches in each nation became self-governing by their own local church structure. In the era of anticolonial feelings in many parts of the world this change was necessary for political reasons. Practical and theological reasons also made it better for the churches in other countries to be self-governing. By assuming their own responsibility for government, the area churches became more aware of their need for national church workers, for financial support of the churches' work, for developing their own mission programs, and for becoming a part of their own culture. The Missouri Synod continued to give subsidies to sister churches and provide church workers to help in special areas such as medical missions or the training of local pastors and teachers.

Work in Korea was begun in 1958 with the view of developing a Korean church that would not first be dependent upon control by Americans and then have to learn to become independent. The Korean Lutheran Church has made outstanding progress and is evidence of the ability of a sister church to function as such from its very beginning.

The mission program also expanded to do more than just found Lutheran congregations. Since 1960 the synod supported a radio ministry in the Middle East which has not begun a new congregation but has broadcast the Gospel of Christ supportive to many scattered Christians in the area.

The sister church relationship with mission fields around the world has also given those churches an opportunity to help the Christians in the United States. Their teachers and theologians also make contributions to the church that had sent them missionaries.

Now for the schools: Would you believe that the synod did not relocate a single synodical school in 25 years? But there were changes. In 1957 the junior college in Fort Wayne became a senior college— and was moved across town. Those who want to become pastors attend one of the junior colleges, then go to Fort Wayne, where they complete work for a bachelors degree. Then they go on to a seminary. Or, by taking special makeup work they can graduate from another college and then enter one of the seminaries.

In 1963 another Concordia College opened—in Ann Arbor, Michigan. In 1961 a Lay Institute was added to the college in Milwaukee as a separate school. Lay people attend the institute for 2 years and are called as lay ministers to serve many functions in a congregation. The St. Paul college became a 4-year school and the Bronxville school will start a 4-year program in 1973. Valparaiso University added a new campus, including a new Deaconess Hall where all the synod's deaconesses are trained. By the way, the Lutheran Deaconess Association received its first woman executive director, Dr. Lucille Wassman, in 1971.

Another office for ministry in congregations developed: directors of Christian education. Both teachers colleges offer special training to men and women to become DCEs. The DCEs work in areas of parish education beyond the Christian day school. Numerous congregations established weekday Christian schools, once-a-week classes after school or on Saturdays. The traditional confirmation classes that had been held for only the 7th and 8th grades have, in many places, become a part of a weekday Christian school that extends instruction down to first grade or lower. Some have also extended weekday classes to high school students and adults.

"Life in Christ" a new Sunday school curriculum was introduced to the synod in 1949. A total new education program for the synod involving coordinated programs for Sunday school, Christian day school, weekday Christian school and vacation Bible school was introduced in 1971. The curriculum "Mission:Life" starts with preschool-age children and goes through adult levels. In 1967 the Concordia Catechism Series, a basic 3-volume series covering Bible history, Luther's Catechism, and worship, with manuals and workbooks, was introduced to the synod to prepare youth for confirmation.

Various social ministries provided by the synod continued to expand. The Missouri Synod became especially known for its work with retarded children, the deaf, and the blind. Besides having Bethesda Lutheran Home and the Good Shepherd Home of the West, both for retarded children, the synod developed educational materials for retarded children. Many congregations operate special Sunday school classes using this material. Since 1967 the synod has had a full-time executive secretary for the commission on Mental Retardation, Marshall Nelson.

The Missouri Synod also has two schools for deaf children and 41 full-time pastors serving deaf congregations. One pastor, William Ludwig, is also deaf. The synod also operates a library for the blind that provides books, Sunday school lessons, and periodicals for blind people. Many volunteers throughout the church use Braille machines to prepare the material for the library.

In 1950 the synod finally brought the social ministries of the church into the synodical structure. Dr. Henry Wind became the first executive secretary of the Board of Social Welfare. He was the grandson of J. F. Buenger, the man who initiated Missouri's social ministries.

The new office of a full-time executive secretary in social ministries was part of an obvious trend for a stronger synodical organization during the fifth 25-year period of Missouri Synod history. The addition of more full-time administrators required more centralized government to coordinate their work. Already in 1941 the synod had approved plans to buy or build a synodical office building. A building was bought at 210 N. Broadway, St. Louis, and dedicated in September 1951. Synod's president, Dr. J. W. Behnken moved his office from Chicago to St. Louis. The treasurer's office and other departments of synod that had been housed at the publishing house also moved to the new building. The synod had 85 full-time staff members, when "210" was dedicated. At last the synod had a building that could be referred to as "the Vatican" or "the Kremlin" in synodical humor.

One of the occupants of the new building was John Herrmann, who in 1950 became the synod's first executive secretary of stewardship. Another synodwide special offering, Conquest for Christ, was held in 1952 to raise money for, among other things, the new senior college at Fort Wayne. The special offering received $13 million, $3 million over its goal. By 1954 the synodical budget reached $8 million. Rather than have regular special offerings (a contradiction in terms) the synod made a Venture of Faith in 1955 to increase the annual offerings to synod. In 1956 synod received $12.9 million; in 1962 the synodical income went over $20 million. In 1967 the synod had another special offering, the first in 15 years. Called Ebenezer, the program asked members to consider giving a special gift on their birthdays. The goal had been to raise $40 million, but the total receipts were $14 million. As the synod nears its 125th anniversary its annual income is around $26 million.

The Church Extension Fund also received a full-time executive secretary. Starting in 1953 the Extension Fund started accepting money on deposit as well as donations. The fund grew to a 1972 balance of $53,750,000 of which $32 million is deposits.

Evangelism received increased attention in the Missouri Synod during the 50s and 60s. Preaching, Teaching, Reaching Missions (known as PTRs and described by some as Lutheran revivals) took off in the early 1950s. Operated on a congregational level, though cooperating on a circuit or area level, the PTRs sent lay callers out into neighborhoods to invite people to special evening services. The services were informal and without the usual Lutheran liturgical involvement.

Building churches for many new congregations received an assist from a growing Church Extension Fund, which provided capital at low rates.

(Mission Education Photo)

Not only did the PTRs bring many more members into the synod, they also helped make lay people more aware of their ability to be evangelists. Other programs with different approaches, such as Spiritual Life Missions and Families for Christ, were also encouraged by the synod. Each had an evangelistic flavor. The number of adults joining the synod reached new heights—over 31,000 in 1954, over 35,000 in 1962. Since then there has been a gradual decline in new adults entering the Missouri Synod—over 26,000 in 1971.

Evangelism was a special department of the Board of Missions until 1971, when it was made a separate board. Dr. Erwin Kolb became the first executive secretary of the board. As part of the 125th anniversary celebration the synod participated in Key 73, a nation-wide evangelism effort involving 140 denominations. Its director, Dr. Theodore A. Raedeke, was a former director of evangelism for the Missouri Synod.

The Lutheran Hour continued to be an important part of both the home and overseas mission effort of the synod. Dr. Maier, The Lutheran Hour speaker since its beginning, died in January 1950. At the time of his death The Lutheran Hour was broadcast over 600 stations in the United States, plus many overseas. Dr. Oswald Hoffmann became the new Lutheran Hour speaker in 1955. He still serves in that capacity in 1972.

The Missouri Synod also began a television ministry in 1952 with "This Is the Life" a half-hour religious drama produced by Dr. Herman Gockel. The stars of "This Is the Life," the Fisher family, and their minister, Pastor Martin, became a part of the Missouri Synod. "This Is the Life" continues to be one of the most widely broadcast religious TV programs, though the Fisher family has been retired in favor of independent dramas. Lutheran Television entered the field of children's cartoon programs in 1970 with "Christmas Is" a story of Benji and his dog, Waldo.

A stewardship movie, *All That I Have*, produced by the Missouri Synod, won a Freedoms Foundation Award in 1953. The major Lutheran synods in the United States worked together to produce *Martin Luther* a full-length movie about the great Reformer. Shown in public theaters throughout the country from 1953 forward, the film reached large audiences. The same group of Lutherans also produced *Question 7* the story of a pastor's family living under communism in Europe.

The Walther League reached its peak of activities during the 1950s. District and International Walther League conventions drew large crowds of young people. Lutheran Service Volunteer Schools,

111

a combination camp and training school for congregational youth activities, were held in the late 50s and early 60s. Caravaners (teams of trained youth) traveled from congregation to congregation to encourage youth activities. The Walther League developed the Prince of Peace Volunteer program through which young people could go to foreign countries to work in mission programs.

A senior Walther League was formed in many areas for those over 18, but most Walther League work was with high school age youth. In 1962 the executive secretary of the Walther League, Elmer Witt, became also the executive secretary of Synod's Board for Young People's Work. In 1965 the synod assumed full responsibility for youth programs within the synodical structure through a board with a new title — Board of Youth Ministries. The Walther League continued as a youth-led, issue-oriented organization, again reaching older youth.

The Lutheran Laymen's League continued its support of The Lutheran Hour and expanded into other radio ministries, "Day by Day with Jesus" and the "Family Worship Hour." The LLL also started another effort to reach people through newspapers, "Preaching through the Press," and gave financial support to "This Is the Life." In 1957 the LLL's membership went over 100,000.

After having rented offices from the publishing house in St. Louis since its beginning, the LLL dedicated its own headquarters building at 2185 Hampton in St. Louis on April 19, 1959.

Though the Lutheran Women's Missionary League was the last to make the Missouri Synod three-team league, it soon became the largest, having a membership of over 200,000. The LWML's mite box projects have helped finance numerous mission projects both in the synod's home and overseas missions. The women are also noted for their Bible study programs and mission emphasis on the congregational level. Some say that LWML means "Let's Witness More, Ladies."

A brief look at publication events in the last 25 years. In 1956 Concordia Publishing House issued the first of 54 volumes of a new English translation of Luther, *Luther's Works*. Copublished with Fortress Press (the LCA's publishing house) this project is to be completed in 1975. In 1958 the Concordia Tract Mission became a part of CPH. Ralph Reinke succeeded O. A. Dorn as general manager of CPH in 1971.

The *Lutheran Witness Reporter* (a newspaper) became a companion publication to the *Lutheran Witness* (a magazine) in 1965. The combined publication reached a circulation of over half a million in the late 60s.

The Missouri Synod did something radically new in 1953 – it held its convention in Houston, Texas. Prior to that time all conventions had been held in Missouri, Ohio, and four other states (Illinois, Indiana, Wisconsin, and Michigan). After 1953 the other states category expanded as conventions were held in St. Paul, San Francisco, New York and Denver. The 1973 convention, which is to conclude the 125th anniversary celebration, will be in New Orleans.

The big events during the years between Missouri Synod's 100th and 125th anniversaries were connected with intra-Lutheran relationships – as they had been in the previous quarter.

After the Missouri Synod declined fellowship with the ALC in 1947, it looked as though the two groups had plotted separate courses. But two years later they were again holding discussions about the possibility of establishing fellowship. By the end of 1949 a joint committee of the two groups had drafted and approved the *Common Confession,* Part I. Both the Missouri Synod and the ALC accepted this new document at their 1950 conventions.

The Missouri Synod then presented the first part of the *Common Confession* to the Synodical Conference. The Synod of Evangelical Lutheran Churches (that used to be the Slovak Synod) accepted it. The Wisconsin Synod and the ELS (formerly the Norwegian Synod) not only rejected it but requested the Missouri Synod to end all talks with the ALC. But by that time the ALC and Missouri were making progress on the last half of the *Common Confession.*

In 1954 the ALC approved the *Common Confession,* Part II. The Synodical Conference convention that year was stormy. The Wisconsin Synod and the ELS renewed their opposition against Missouri's discussions with the ALC. Missouri delayed approval of the final half of the *Common Confession* until 1956 with the hope of keeping peace in the Synodical Conference.

But by then it was too late to establish fellowship with the ALC because it had worked out merger plans with the three other synods in the American Lutheran Conference to form The American Lutheran Church (note the new church body is The ALC, replacing the ALC). The American Lutheran Church completed its organization in 1960. Since it was a new group, discussions about fellowship would have to start over.

At the 1959 Missouri Synod convention in San Francisco, Committee No. 3 (Doctrinal Matters) presented Resolution No. 9 to adopt the *Brief Statement* as part of the public doctrine of the Missouri Synod. Though the Brief Statement had been approved back in 1932, its position was not clear. Resolution No. 9 passed. This could have ended all fellowship discussions because it gave the Missouri Synod a different list of confessional statements than other Lutheran bodies.

But three years later in Cleveland, Resolution No. 9 of the previous convention was declared unconstitutional. Doctrinal statements cannot be adopted by a convention because new statements would require a constitution change. The Brief Statement was removed from its "official" position in the Missouri Synod. However, the previous synodical resolutions approving the Brief Statement remain on the synodical record.

In 1962 the United Lutheran Church, the Augustana Lutheran Church, and two smaller groups formed the Lutheran Church in America (LCA). (About that time there was another move to change Missouri Synod's name. Some suggested calling it The Lutheran Church—American Synod, which would really have confused everyone). The two mergers forming the ALC and the LCA left the National Lutheran Council with only two members.

Meetings were held between The ALC, the LCA, the SELC [Synod of Evangelical Lutheran Churches] and the Missouri Synod to determine the possibility of forming a new Lutheran council. The four synods formed the Lutheran Council in the United States of America (LCUSA), and the Missouri Synod approved its membership at the Detroit convention in 1965. For the first time in American history about 95% of all Lutherans were united in a common council. Though basically they were still divided on the same three lines as of over 100 years before—General Synod, General Council, and Synodical Conference—they now had a forum for mutual study and a place to cooperate in missions, social ministry, and other special needs. Membership in the council did not imply fellowship in the Lutheran usage of the term.

The Missouri Synod had new alliances in LCUSA but the Synodical Conference was falling apart. The Wisconsin Synod and the ELS wanted to disband the Synodical Conference, but Missouri and SELC refused. All of the Synodical Conference congregations in the South had become a part of the Southern District of the Missouri Synod in 1961. At the same time a number of ALC congregations in southern black communities also became a part of the Missouri Synod. The ALC had no white congregations in the area. The black congregations could more easily become a part of a Lutheran community in the Missouri Synod.

In 1964 the National Evangelical Lutheran Church joined the Missouri Synod. The NELC was a small synod of Finnish background that had been in altar and pulpit fellowship with Missouri since 1923.

Every time the Wisconsin Synod had a convention there were resolutions urging it to withdraw from the Synodical Conference. When it refused, a group left Wisconsin and formed a more conservative synod. The ELS did not wait for Wisconsin but went ahead to withdraw its membership from the Synodical Conference and end all relationships with Missouri. In 1963 by a vote of 138 to 28 the Wisconsin Synod also left the Synodical Conference. With only two members left (Missouri and SELC) the Synodical Conference was dissolved in 1967 at the age of 95.

Meanwhile talks between the Missouri Synod and The American Lutheran Church regarding fellowship were established. The 1967 convention in Detroit (the last to be held every third year) referred the fellowship issue to the districts and opened the door for acceptance in 1969.

Fellowship was the big issue at the 1968 district conventions of the Missouri Synod. Delegates at one district convention, apparently unaware of the long history of fellowship talks, pleaded for a delay in voting on fellowship because they had not had time to study the matter. That request prompted the convention to consider, but not pass, the following resolution:

WHEREAS our Lord has promised that He will come soon to judge the earth;

WHEREAS His proposed action will have tremendous effect upon the church; and

WHEREAS the church has not had time to prepare for this great event;

Be it Resolved that the church petition the Lord to delay His coming for two more years, and

Be it Finally Resolved that each district appoint an executive secretary of eschatology (that is, last things) who will be responsible for making final preparations for the promised event.

In 1969 the synodical convention of the Missouri Synod meeting in Denver declared altar and pulpit fellowship with The American Lutheran Church.

Though resolutions to the 1971 convention in Milwaukee questioned both Missouri's membership in the Lutheran Council and the fellowship with the ALC, both relationships remained intact.

Other actions at the 1969 convention altered the activities of Missouri Synod congregations. Women were given the right to vote in congregational meetings. The question of women's suffrage had always been a difficult one. The issue was never considered a doctrine but always a custom that was unwritten but somehow official. Following the Denver convention there was a rash of Missouri Synod news items about "The First Woman to . . ." to hold various congregation offices, to be a delegate to a district convention, to hold a district office, to vote at a synodical convention. Pastors had to make hurried changes when they inducted their church council. No longer could they say, "Dear Brothers."

The Denver convention also introduced the *Worship Supplement* to the Missouri Synod. With additional hymns and orders of worship the supplement was an additional worship resource, while discussions were held about a joint Lutheran hymnal. Other new worship orders and songs have been prepared and tested since. Those in a Missouri Synod worship service in 1972, like those in 1847, often find themselves using more than one hymnal.

No one knows for sure when the first Missouri Synod pastor wore a clerical collar, but all agree that it must have happened "out East." In 1947 the backward collar would have been cause of serious suspicions about a pastor's theology. In 1972 the average Missouri Synod church member would be surprised to see the pastor in the pulpit without a clerical collar.

In addition to the collar the typical parish pastor wears a black cassock covered with a white surplice and a stole when he leads worship. There are still some wearing a Geneva robe. But then there are also some who are wearing full Eucharistic vestments with alb and chasuble.

The altars in new churches (and those remodeled recently) are out from the wall again. Only this time the pastor stands behind the altar during part of the service rather than turn his back to the congregation.

Most congregations have the Lord's Supper, some now call it the Eucharist, at least twice a month, some every Sunday. Some congregations are giving first Communion to young people at an earlier age, about 10, before they are confirmed. Some are confirming youth later (end of the 10th grade), but most are still confirmed at the end of the 8th grade.

Most congregations have had a number of "folk masses" by 1972. Most Missourians have been able to accept and even to enjoy an occasional guitar—except maybe those who contributed over $100 to the new organ fund. Banners became commonplace in most of the synod's congregations during the late 60s.

Missouri, you've come a long way.

X. Synod and Grace
(Or "Across the Wide Missouri")

The tour is over. But if we have achieved any of the objectives suggested in the first chapter, there should be some applications in the last chapter. As promised, the answers are not in the back of the book. Rather there are some questions – and evaluations – that relate the history of the synod to the synod today and (admitting the limitations of human prophecy) the synod of tomorrow.

Question No. 1: Has the Missouri Synod changed?

Of course it has. If the synod had not changed in some areas it would not be here to celebrate its 125th anniversary. On the other hand, if it had changed in other areas it wouldn't be here either. For a corporate body to continue to live it must both change and remain unchanged. The challenge is to know when to do which.

It is easy to agree that some things must be changed and some remain unchanged. But it is foolish to assume that everyone will agree on a division of ideas into the two categories. The history of the synod shows a constant tension among people as they face the issue of change. Some have zealously watched the doctrines and traditions to keep the synod on the track. (Would you call them conservatives?) With equal zeal some have plunged into society to use the doctrines and to keep the synodical train moving. (Would you call them liberals?) The point is that the train had to both stay on the track and to keep moving to be of value.

The 125 years of continuous existence of the same church body makes both change and the lack of it highly visible in the Missouri Synod. Only one Lutheran group in the United States, the Eielsen Synod, is older than the Missouri Synod, and it has only 2,000 baptized members – the size of one large Missouri Synod congregation. All the other Lutheran groups have gone through various mergers, deaths, resurrections, and the like. In so doing they have had the opportunity to drop the embarrassing parts of their history. The out-of-date and

incorrect positions are never a part of the new group. But Missouri has had to live with her mistakes. Part of the price of keeping the good parts of history (if one also wants to be honest) is to keep the less pleasant parts also. The advantages of keeping an organizational history outweigh the disadvantages. It shows that the forefathers had a concept of church that kept their structure flexible enough to change as the world changed and yet stable enough to remain intact. The Missouri Synod of 1973 owes the same consideration to the generations that follow.

Question No. 2: How does The Lutheran Church—Missouri Synod stack up as a denomination? What kind of rating should it get for 125 years on the American church scene?

Missouri Synod Lutherans like to rate themselves highly. Their publications and news relases often point out that they have been the fastest growing Lutheran group for years, their offerings are the highest per member in denominations with over a million members, and their education requirements are the highest—both for church workers and members. Though the Missouri Synod is small among the tribes of America (slightly more than 1.3% of the population) it operates one of the larger religious publishing houses, has two of the larger Protestant seminaries, has the largest Protestant parochial school system, and sponsors a radio and a TV program that are among the oldest religious programs on the air. After pausing for breath, some Missourians could add to the list.

But these achievements are seen more realistically (and actually seem more worthwhile) when looked at in their historical development. If the "pointing with pride" part of a synodical evaluation does not also look at failures—both failures to succeed and failures to try—then the boasting fails to understand the true nature of the church on earth and also fails to use success as a way to develop others.

It's easier to talk about Conquest for Christ, a special drive that went $3 million over its goal; than Ebenezer that fell $26 million short.

It's easier to promote Walther as a hero than Stephan; though both were equally sinful and equally forgiven by the theology they taught and believed. It's easier to explain the success of the Lutheran Church in Korea than the failure among the Indians in Michigan. It's easier to report every year that the synod ended the year with the books in the black (which they always do in recent years) than to list what didn't get done because there were no funds left. Synod's educational system makes better public relations copy than its history of the treatment of minority groups.

Naturally, success gets more attention than failure because it lasts longer. The mission field that stays open stays in the public eye. The one that failed is forgotten. Many other denominations that existed or began 125 years ago are not celebrating in 1972 for the simple reason that they did not survive.

But had the synod started programs only if they were sure of success, nothing would have happened. The failures are also important. They show people were willing to try. Program failures show that a different approach must be used — not that the effort was wrong. Human failures show that someone tried to do more than he was able to do — not necessarily that he was wrong.

Synod's record for its first 125 years must reflect not how it succeeded or how it failed, but how it lived with either event. If failures made it afraid to try again, or if successes made it rest on its record, the synod deserves censure. But if failures made it try harder, and successes encouraged it to do more, it rates approval. The degree of rating is not important — except that members of the synod in 1972 should be aware of the appraisal, since their present activity will be reflected in the future.

Question No. 3: Are there two Missouri Synods? Is there a conservative/liberal or an orthodox/evangelical division?

Polarization is one of the "in" theological words of 1972 — not only in the Missouri Synod, but in other denominations — not only in churches but also in society. To deny that there is polarization in the Missouri Synod in its 125th year would be deliberate deceit at its worst or innocent ignorance at its best.

But there is no reason to be polarized about polarization. The term may be new, but the concept is not. Even a quick look at the synod's history shows there were no "good old days" when everything went right. There has always been conflict. This does not mean that conflict is good and that we need to keep things stirred up. The important issues are: What is the conflict about? And how do those in conflict treat one another?

Imagine a teeter-totter. When the group that formed the Missouri Synod 125 years ago got together, they balanced the seesaw of their new synod by huddling together at the spot they declared to be the middle. The huddle in the middle was nice for a balanced teeter-totter, but it also required that all work be done in the middle — the area they had chosen. As the synod reached out into new areas — new ministries, new people, new cultures — there was danger of throwing itself out of balance. But not as long as it reached out in both directions.

If the synod became more exact in its theology and at the same time more involved in using that theology in the world, the teeter-totter stayed in balance. But if theological exactness became the only goal, the ministry part suffered. (Remember how we used to get the heavier kids on one end of the seesaw and shake up the lighter kid on the other — it works in theology too.) Or if all the weight were put on action and theology were ignored, the board would go out of balance in the other direction.

The synod has not always kept its teeter-totter in balance. But it seems to be aware of the need for a balance. There are polarized positions in the synod that stay on one side or the other of the synodical seesaw. But there also seems to be a third group — a group that seems willing to put its weight on the side that needs help in keeping the balance.

There should be and often is a healthy respect for those on the far-out positions. If someone were not concerned about solid theology, many exciting new ministries couldn't exist. If others weren't willing to live on the edge of the seesaw that reaches into challenging and unknown areas there would be no need for all that good theology. To rejoice in mercy together there need be no big rush to the center of the teeter-totter. But there needs to be a greater awareness of how the balance is maintained. No individual should see his own position as the only right one and try to get everyone to rush to his spot.

One of the reasons that the synod has polarization is that its members are aware that they are all on the same seesaw. They yell at each other because they know the other guy might throw things out of balance. Perhaps more than other denominations Missouri Synod members feel joint ownership. That is our college and seminary, watch out what you do to it. That is our mission field so don't do your thing to our thing. It is good to have peace in a family but not the kind of peace achieved by everyone going his own way and ignoring the rest. Maybe it is putting a strain on Luther's advice to "put the best construction on everything," but at least the brothers and sisters in the Missouri Synod aren't ignoring one another.

Many events in the synod's history show how its balance was lost and regained. The early fathers kept the German language so they could keep their balance in a new culture. But the same hanging on to the German later threw the synod off balance because the issues had changed. There was no longer a danger of losing their theology, but the protection was kept to safeguard something that no longer needed protection.

Today some want to keep every doctrine of the church in the same words and phrases that have been used in times past. They know the meaning of those words and are sure that true doctrine is being taught as long as the reliable words are used.

Others say that to keep the same doctrine new words must be used. Old words sometimes develop new shades of meaning. Unless the words are changed to present-day meanings, the doctrine may be changed, not by the mouth of the speaker, but by the ears of the hearer.

The synod must be concerned about maintaining a balance—not balance as an average that pleases everybody—but a balance that keeps the synod on a level where it can do its work rather than struggle with itself to get into position to work.

Since liberal and conservative are the common measuring stick in theological as well as political circles, we must take a look at polarization in those terms. But it should be said that in the total church picture the liberal/conservative scale is not a good measuring system. To illustrate, change your mental image from a teeter-totter to a long street that crosses town. Call it Grand. Address on Grand Street also shows the location: 24 North Grand is near center, 3517 North Grand is far north; 4216 South Grand is even farther south.

Now see theology as such a street: 24 Liberal Theology is near center, as is 24 Conservative Theology; 3517 Conservative Theology is far out conservative; 4216 Liberal Theology is way out liberal. All Missouri Synod Lutherans live on Conservative Theology when measured on the total scale. It is only when we compare ourselves to each other that we notice the numerical difference. (For example, the person living at 4543 South Grand sees the house at 4317 South Grand as being north even though it is far south—but it is still north of 4543 South Grand.) When you hear synodical name calling, remember that we're just talking about the people on our block—not the entire street.

The polarization situation must also be related to issues. One must be liberal about or conservative about something. Such positions require objects. Lutherans are conservative on the doctrine of Christ—Christ is the God-man who gave salvation to all people. Such a conservative position must make one liberal on the subject of race because Christ is the Savior of all people, so all people are our brothers and sisters. Lutherans are conservative about the Scripture. It is God's Word. Because they know God has spoken (conservative view) they can be sure of His action in Christ. Therefore they can have a free life-style (liberal view).

An understanding of the relationship of broader views is an important task for the coming years of the synod. All answers will not be found by looking into the last 125 years. But the presence of these broader views can be seen in the synod's history. All, not just one, of the views have contributed to the strength of the synod.

Question No. 4: What is the future of The Lutheran Church—Missouri Synod?

There is an easy, though simple and rather pious sounding answer. The Holy Spirit will continue to work through the synod to the same extent that the synod is open to the power of the Gospel of Jesus Christ. Or in simpler words: Jesus won't cop out on us.

The answer is less simple and less pious sounding if seen in the light of history. The power of the Spirit has always been evident in the synod (but never only in the synod, just in case anyone still thinks that way). But in the future as in the past the presence of the Spirit does not mean that all conflict and all difficulties are gone. It is not true that if one is doing the Lord's work everything goes right. The world being what it is, and the church being a part of the world, making it a part of the problem too, we can be sure that conflicts and difficulties will remain.

But the promise of the Gospel is that we won't face those troubles alone. We are united in Jesus Christ. That is a union with a future, a predictable future.

For Further Reading

Why stop now? This book is offered as an introduction to the history of The Lutheran Church—Missouri Synod. Since you made it through the introduction, you might like to study a special section or a more complete overview of the Synod's history. Below are some recommendations.

First, there are three other books in this series for the 125th anniversary of the Missouri Synod. *Love Leaves Home* gives a more detailed history of Wilhelm Loehe. *Walther Writes to the Church* is a collection of Walther's letters. The letters will help you understand Walther as a person and the issues of his day. *God's Yes and God's No* is a condensed version of Walther's most famous book *Law and Gospel.*

Next some books available through Concordia Publishing House, though they are also often found in church or a pastor's library.

A Century of Grace was published for the centenial of the Missouri Synod. Now available in paperback, it gives a detailed history of the synod, including names of missionaries, professors, and synodical leaders. By W. A. Baepler.

Life in Two Worlds is a biography of Wilhelm Sihler. By L Spitz.

Moving Frontiers is a collection of documents, letters, proceedings, and other original sources of the history of Lutheranism in America with a special emphasis on the Missouri Synod. Collected by Carl S. Meyer, who also edited *Letters of C. F. W. Walther: A Selection,* it is similar to the other book in this series but with different letters.

For the history of parochial schools read *Schools of The Lutheran Church—Missouri Synod* by A. C. Stellhorn.

Log Cabin to Luther Tower, by Carl S. Meyer, is the history of Concordia Seminary in St. Louis. *College with a Cause* is the history of Concordia Teachers College, River Forest, Illinois, from 1864 to 1964. By A. Freitag.

The Life of Dr. C. F. W. Walther, by Lewis Spitz is a history of the most famous of the founders of the Missouri Synod.

Several districts of the Synod have published histories. *The Heart of Missouri,* by August Suelflow, is about the old Western District (which has now divided into 19 districts, so the history covers a large section of Missouri Synod); *Faith to Move Mountains,* by L. Schafer, the history of the Colorado District.

Teach My People the Truth is the story of Frankenmuth, Michigan, by Herman F. Zehnder; available through the author at Box 404, Frankenmuth, Michigan 48734.

Several important history books are out of print. They are listed here not to frustrate the reader but to encourage you to check your church library and ask your pastor if he has a copy.

Zion on the Mississippi, by Walter O. Forster, is the most complete history of the Saxon migration to Perry County.

Which Way to Lutheran Unity? by John H. Tietjen, traces the relationship of large and small Lutheran groups as they merge and divide.

Light in the Dark Belt, by Rosa Young, tells the story of a young black woman in the South and her work in the Lutheran Church.

We Move into Africa, by Henry Nau, is the story of the first Lutheran mission work in Nigeria, written by the first missionary.